I dedicate this book to my one and only daughter La'Shyra Thomas who has always looked to me with a certain hope in her eyes. I hope I have restored your faith in me as a woman. I've made some decisions that ultimately ended in our suffering and I've failed at putting you first in all times so again, I apologize. It is my prayer that you take my lessons and pain in life and use it as a strategy to overcome the enemy's plots against you especially concerning love. I wish you joy, much peace, more wisdom and a love that exceeds your wildest dreams. My greatest contribution to this world has nothing to do with what I've done or who I am but it has everything to do with you. I am so proud of who you are, remember the world is your oyster! I love you so much!

To my mom Dorothy (my hero) I have no words that could express my gratitude for EVERYTHING that you've done for me. I am a blessed woman because of you. I honor you forever my queen. To my dad Tyrone who has been the epitome of a great hard working man and the BEST FATHER a girl could ask for, I honor you my King. To my big sister Kenya, THANK YOU for being my friend & my protector...for loving & caring for me without judging me...You inspire me in so many ways. It was during my toughest times that you three have been an anchor for me and I appreciate you ALL so much.

To my mentor Elder Evelyn Mann-Carter, I want to thank you for your obedience to God. You have taken me under your wings of wisdom and shown me a great Christian example as a woman of God. You are truly his disciple and a light to me.

To my abusers, I forgive you... To those that I've abused I hope that you can find it in your heart to forgive me too.

To my lord and savior Jesus Christ, Thank you for loving me..It is your perfect love towards me that gives me strength from day to day. You saved my soul and you resuscitated my life, I love you and I am forever grateful.

To my nephews (3 kings) Phillip Jr., Kendall (Champ) & Khristian. I pray Gods love, protection and guidance over your lives. You will be great successful leaders one day.

To my 3 angels; Tyrone Hearn (dad), Phillip (brother) & Julian (nephew) continue to rest in heaven until we meet again.

-Pre-Face-

I almost collapsed! I stood as firmly as I could on one leg, feeling myself fall to the ground. I tried to gently lay myself down in the drive way, my right leg was hanging on by threads of flesh. I felt the blood flowing out of my body similar to that of a fountain. I could see and feel my clothes being saturated with my blood, it felt warm and wet. I couldn't believe what had just happened, I looked down and I saw my arm seemingly deformed and hanging over my chest on a limb. The shock of it all could've killed me, I was so scared. I remember crying out "Oh Jesus" not even knowing what to say next but my spirit was in pain and groaned for me, as I thought to myself "Why did I come here?" then I heard God whisper in my ear "you're going to be okay" All of sudden I felt a peace come over me as if the world had just paused for a second. I was as calm as I could possibly be. I continued to lay in silence and it seemed as if moments had gone by before I heard movement again but that was just me going in and out of consciousness.

    He handed this young lady her purse and said "here, baby girl you can just leave." I saw her shadow as she stood nearby & I heard her footsteps as she walked away. His next words were "See I told you!" followed by "Oh my God, what have I done!" then he came closer and said to me "come on baby just get up, please, let's go in the house" as he tugged at my arm that was dismantled. I replied "No, don't touch me, that hurts." I asked him to call the ambulance but he acted as if I didn't say a thing and he continued to pace over me and talk to himself. "My life is over now, I'm about to kill myself" he said. "No don't say that." I said to him and he quickly rebutted "Yes, I am, what am I supposed to do now?" Again, I asked "Please call the ambulance, don't let me die here, please" again no answer but still he paced around me and mumbled words to himself.

    I laid there trying to come up with a story to tell the cops if they arrived, I didn't want him to get into any trouble. One of his worst fears was going back to prison & I could hear the despair in his voice, he went from angry to afraid. I heard the sirens from afar, it seemed as if they were getting closer. I've never been so happy to hear sirens in my life. It was a sound of relief. I could hear voices and footsteps in the grass then I heard an officer say "we have a female laid in the driveway she appears to be conscious oh wait I have a male here" and bang! Before the officer could finish his sentence...It was over!
How did I get to this place?

Life Lesson 1 – No Kiss Goodbye!

Not sure what time he crept in the house that night but it was late in the a.m. hour and I had waited up long enough. In and out of sleep and In and out of prayer was my routine anytime my husband was not where he was supposed to be, lying next to me. My husband and I had somehow become two separate individuals on two totally different paths. It was a heck of an adjustment because at one point in our lives we were one in the same. We were both out here thuggin' well more so carelessly living life but then my life took shift and I started to get serious about salvation and my relationship with God. I was suddenly interested in holiness and that sparked a change in everything around me.

We were young, teenage parents and high school sweethearts. I was 20 years old when he asked me to be his wife and he was just 21. It was the most precious moment. We sat inside of an Italian restaurant on Valentine's Day, a table for two. He was so nervous about the whole proposal that he invited a mutual friend to come along for his support. After dinner Rico got down on one knee inside of the restaurant in front of all these strangers as they starred on to see what would happen next, he began to mumble words that I'm still not sure of to this day. All I heard was the noise of everyone chanting him on. I do know that he asked me to marry him and of course I said yes, so we got married.

As a young couple we were doing the best we could with what we had and what we had was enough if only we had realized it at the time. We were so use to hard roads that I guess it was difficult to recognize any easier routes but we were blessed indeed to say the least. My husband had a good paying job. I worked part time and went to school myself. We had our own place and we were making our own way trying to rid any negativity in our path. Don't get me wrong, we weren't horrible people but we were missing aim, we had no real focus or purpose and that's what I got from God. I received wisdom, instruction and hope whenever I encountered Gods presence and the more I kept in his presence the more I received Gods love, mercy and grace. I changed a lot of my old habits and certain ways of thinking. I was living a married with children life and everything I did in those days was based around the church.

Monday nights were praise team rehearsals, Tuesday Night was Bible Study, Thursday was Choir Rehearsal and Sunday was worship and repeat, the rest of my time was spent with family, loving on my kids or interceding for my husband.

My husband was a good man, an excellent provider and protector of us all but that same loving and loyal nature that he had with his family he also had with his not so loyal friends in the streets. I could feel us slowly drifting apart. Rico never wanted to go to church with me and our girls after work he was either at home or on the block. I knew one day God would get a hold of him and we would begin to walk purposely in our purpose together at least that was my vision. We were the best of friends still, he withheld nothing from me and vice versa. We loved each other so much. I never doubted his love for me and I never had to question his motives or his word and that's what I loved about him the most. He kept every promise he ever made to me but of course like any other marriage we had our not so good days but overall he was a good husband & I was truly committed to being the best wife I could be and I stopped at nothing in the spirit realm to make sure I covered him in prayer. Although it seemed the more I prayed the more he would go back to the hood and hang out in the streets and the more susceptible he became to what the streets had to offer. The streets had become his downfall, sort of like guilty by association.

My husband Rico and I shared a lot of common traits. We both believed in respect, trust and integrity above all. Things began to change drastically for us after this one night, we were approached by a slow moving vehicle on 6 mile (a really busy street) where I grew up, it was just getting dark out and this car slowly rode up on us as we were getting out of our car visiting my parents. It was Me, Rico & our daughter. I remember feeling like something wasn't right, a bit scared as he told us to quickly go inside the house. I hurried inside as I heard this guy say "skinny man, what's up?" as the passenger window rolled down. Rico walked up to the car to talk to this person and I'm not sure what was said but he came inside seemingly frustrated, later on I find out just who this guy was and what his intentions were with my husband that night.

Rico had just become friends with this individual named Vince and they started to hang out more & more. Vince was a known drug dealer and Rico was a working man who hustled on the side, why they were getting so close? I don't know but I knew a lot of people wanted Rico around because he was muscle. I'm not sure what happened between the two but it was Vince that pulled up that night. He later revealed to my husband by phone conversation that he intended on killing him that night and because he saw his daughter and girl with him he decided not to, as to give him a pass or something but he clearly wanted to warn Rico that he had an issue with him about whatever.

One thing about Rico he was never one to operate in fear, he was a stand up guy but he wasn't one to play with either, not about us. Rico played it cool and chopped up his differences with Vince for the sake of peace but what he did just didn't sit right with Rico. Vince started to get wind of how unhappy Rico was with him and he knew he had made a big mistake by telling Rico that and was now afraid that my husband would retaliate. Vince drove a silver colored corvette and by coincidence a similar styled corvette was shot up outside of a party one night on the eastside. There were two black men inside this vehicle and one did not survive the gunshot wounds.

People began to talk about the shooting suspecting the deceased individual was Vince because he was in a silver corvette but the person who was murdered was someone that nobody from our neighborhoods even knew. The rumors continued to circulate fast and supposedly Vince was now in fear for his life thinking that my husband was out to get him. He told the police that he thought my husband tried to kill him that night but killed someone else by mistake. I don't know what else he told them but they were now looking for Rico. My husband and I couldn't believe it, the audacity of this man to now make up a story about mistaken identity because he was afraid. He should've known that if my husband was looking to retaliate against him, he would've gotten the right person. I'm not sure why things happen the way that they do but despite my husband's alibi, we knew this was a serious allegation and we also knew how crooked some cops could be so I was afraid. My husband had his run-ins with the authorities so he was not trying to get railroaded by a crooked system.

    I couldn't fast or pray enough. I was splashing anointing oil all over the house, you name it, I did it. Everything started to happen so fast but it was very clear to me that the enemy was at work and this would be the first of many battles to come. I had some Christian friends believing God with me and for my family. I laid at the altar many of days and I cried out unto the lord many of nights because one thing I understood is my position as a wife and I believed that my husband would be sanctified, made holy by me. My relationship with God grew stronger, communication between me and the father was evident. I learned the true unadulterated word of God as I sat under the leadership of a very capable man of God so I was confident in his word and promises towards me and my family.

    I didn't know what to expect but I had so much faith in God that somehow with everything around us beginning to unravel and head toward a dead end I believed that the weapons of our warfare were not carnal but they were mighty through God to the pulling down of strongholds. This chaotic situation was going to be used for Gods Glory somehow. It was time to strap up with the full armor of God it was all we needed to stand against the wiles of the devil.

    The police had come to my parent's house looking for Rico, they had the entire house surrounded by cop cars and cops. They came banging on the front door, the neighbors were coming out looking and wondering what was going on. A few officers greet my mother as she opened the door being the only one home at the time. "Ma'am we're looking for Rico," My mom said to them "he's not here, he doesn't live here" and they asked for permission to search inside my parent's home saying that this was his last known address. My mother told them "No they couldn't, they needed to come back with a search warrant if they wanted to come inside her home" and they left but not before handed my mom a business card asking if she could help her son in law out by letting him know that they were looking for him about a murder that took place at a black party in the city and asked her to call the detective if she found out of his whereabouts. My mom is no joke and although embarrassed by the scene made in front of her home. She wasn't timid or willing to cooperate. All of this about a black party, black party was right because it was about to get real dark and I'm not speaking about the time of the day.

My husband had become a dark individual. He had started popping pills and smoking more. He would come home at times a very different person and at times I was afraid. He and I began to argue a lot and the plot thickened. Back to the night of November 30th 2004 when Rico came home, He didn't get in the bed that night, he crept right to the couch not wanting to make a sound to wake me but I never slept hard when he was away. It had to be around 7am in the morning when I remember being awakened by loud bangs at the door and no these weren't your ordinary bangs that you would hear from a friend "let me in" these were distinctive "trouble is on the other side" police type of bangs. "Open up, It's the police." I heard a voice say as I wiped the sleep from my eyes. I rushed to our girl's room to get them up. I told them to come with me to the bathroom and at 7 and 5 years of age they asked no questions they just followed me with a very scared look on their faces.

I closed the door on them and told them to stay away from the door. I wanted them out of sight because I was afraid of what could possibly happen next. Growing up I had this perception of the police and at the forefront of my mind was that you just don't trust them. I've seen within my family and I've heard within my neighborhood of the crookedness of cops. Little did I know I was about to experience it all first-hand. The bangs at the door continued they turned into kicks and eventually a large object to the door where the door was knocked down. So many officers came rushing in with their guns drawn and seemingly anger in their eyes. Never showing a warrant but walking through our home looking around and asking me and my husband's grandmother (who was also there at the time) where my husband was? We're looking for Rico, where is he? They searched from room to room in our small 2 bedroom apartment they were furious that they did not find my husband. Going to the bathroom door with their guns drawn I immediately yelled out that my girls were in there & to please allow me to get them but the officers just opened the door guns pointed. My two little girls were seen in a corner hugging on each other, guns visibly out they instructed my girls out of the bathroom into the living room where myself and grandma were. "Everybody to the floor NOW!" They told us all to lie down, face to the carpet and not to make one move and so we did.

Laid down next to our girls with my face to the floor, I felt so helpless and ashamed as if I couldn't protect my own children. The officers were getting even the more frustrated because they had been watching our apartment for the past 3 hours or so after receiving a solid tip on where to find Rico so they were obviously confused. They knew they saw my husband enter the apartment really late at night but never saw him exit so they knew he had to still be inside. "Where is he?" They began to yell at me in particularly. All I could think about was a previous conversation that I had with my husband regarding the police showing up. He kept telling me "Tee, I ain't going to jail for something I ain't do, they gon' have to kill me because I ain't going"... even though in a joking manner, I kept those words in the back of my mind. My husband could be a bit fearless and I knew it. I told him to stop talking ignorant, we had a plan to save up enough money for a defense attorney so that he could clear his name and then we suspected all of this would go away.

The police continued to yell at me, "where did he go?" I'm grabbed from off the floor by a female officer and taken to my dining room table area, in efforts to gain my trust. She attempts to have a one on one with me speaking calmly to gain my trust telling me to have a seat and that she wanted to help us but she needed my help first. She then said "look, we know your husband is in here, tell us where he is so that we can leave, once we get him we will leave." I told them once again, "I do not know where he is." All of a sudden I hear an officer yell from our bedroom, "I found him! This motherfucker is in the wall." Must've been the movement that gave it away but my husband had crawled in a hole that was in our bedrooms closet and had he not moved they would've never found him. I wish he would've never moved but he did and some of the officers went rushing into the room and I heard an officer say "Stop resisting before I blow your motherfucking head off!" All I could hear are rumbles and my heart just dropped. I lost my cool for a second, thinking please don't kill my husband in here. I jumped up from the chair at the table and started screaming "No, Please, don't hurt him, please!" I was immediately tackled down to the floor by the female officer and then handcuffed.

My husband is now walking towards the living room accompanied by the officers with his hands handcuffed behind his back, no shirt on just jeans, no belt, socks or shoes. The girls are now crying aloud after seeing their dad being taken away. They were looking at us both in despair as we are motionless, both mother and father handcuffed in front of our small children, Imagine that. I saw a look in my husband's eyes that I had never seen before as he asked the officer "Before you take me, can I give my daughters a kiss?" and the officer replied "No, it's time to go!" Just let me kiss my girls, man.. again he said...."No.. Let's GO!" The officers briefly spoke to one another about what they would do with me. Detroit Police said you can let her go or do what you want to do with her we got who we were looking for & thank you for your assistance. Clinton Township Police said "Okay ma'am you are under arrest for interfering with police duties." I looked on in total disbelief, "Really? you're going to take me to jail in front of my kids." She told me to shut up and I told her "you shut up, you just couldn't leave empty handed, didn't feel accomplished enough as an officer huh." I went on and on and on because I was shocked that they would decide to take me in to custody. In my eyes I never interfered with anything. I answered all their questions.

Grandma was still on the living room floor, not moving. I felt so bad that she had to be humiliated in this way as an elder but we had to leave our girls with grandma while my husband and I were on our way to the department of corrections. Rico was being taken to Wayne County Jail in Detroit and me to Macomb County Jail, the county in which we resided. I must've run my mouth way too much because by the time we had pulled up to the jail and I'm fingerprinted. I'm being charged with Obstruction of Justice and Accessory after the fact of a felony. I wasn't too sure what those charges meant exactly but I knew that once I was able to post bond I would be able to get out and the charges would be dropped. I had a husband to focus on and what was going on with him was most important. With us both being in jail it was hard to communicate with one another but he sent a message to me wanting to know if I was okay and telling me not to worry that the truth would prevail.

--Let no corrupting talk come out of your mouths but only such as is good for building up, as fits the occasion, that it may give grace to those who hear----Ephesians 4:29

    I made my courtesy call to my mom to make sure the girls were with her, safe and okay. She assured me that they would be fine, my brother had picked them up from grandma and they were right there with her and they were good. The entire family was there; my mom and dad, brother & sister included. They all sent me encouragement & strengthening words over the phone. I couldn't eat lunch that day, I didn't even think about dinner, I didn't even drink of water. Just me and my thoughts until the morning comes. Court in the morning and I couldn't wait to see my family. I waited up all night for the next day to come. It was the longest night ever. I stepped into this small spaced room and was told to look at the camera and listen to the judge and reply. I knew that I was about to be released. They advised me of the charges that were against me and I was asked to enter a plea. I was given a court appointed defense attorney who came to get me moments before going to the video arraignment so I had no idea what was to be expected. I told my lawyer that I didn't do anything I was simply just afraid of what would happen to my husband in our apartment that day and he told me that we didn't need to discuss the details just yet, this was just for me to plead guilty or not guilty. My attorney never spoke to me about much of anything even the fact that my family were there in the courtroom waiting to bring me home. I couldn't see anyone in this small room. The judge read off my charges and asked what would I like to plea and I said "I'd like to plead not guilty your honor." I was facing up to 7 years in prison for opening up my mouth. I asked my attorney to ask him about a bond. The judge sets a bond for 100,000 cash or surety, Unbelievable. The judge said that the charges against me were very serious, disregarding the fact that I had never been in any kind of serious trouble before with the law neither was I threat to not appear back in court, he made his decision and asked no questions about it so I was taken back into custody. I was so heart-broken, I knew for sure I was coming home but instead they set a pre-trial date and sent me back to the holding cell. I didn't appreciate the lack of communication with my attorney he was totally detached from my case nor did he listen to my side of the story so I requested another attorney. I got a new female attorney she seemed to be a little more sensitive. --Though I walk in the midst of trouble, you preserve my life; you stretch your hand against the wrath of my enemies, and your right hand delivers me --Psalms 138:7

Meanwhile Rico and I were plastered all over the local news and on the cover of the Clinton township newspaper as if we were these stoned cold criminals. Embarrassed to say the least, I'm a choir member for crying out loud. Here's to singing a new song. It just got real. I was now being processed as an inmate of Macomb county jail I received my number, my uniform and my reality check for sure. I called home again and I talked to my mom on the phone, of course saddened by everything that was going on. I got teary eyed & began to cry over the phone explaining to my mom how unfair this was and telling her I just wanted to come home and be with my daughters. The words spoken next pierced my soul and got me right back on track. Raised by an Alpha woman, my mother is queen of queens and her strength is unmatched. Mom told me "Baby, I know you want to come home and you know if I could bail you out right now, I would but for now you have to be there. You suck those tears up, you're at the wrong place to be showing any weakness, don't you ever let them see you in this way. Hold your head up and pray like you always do. You know your daughter will be well taken care of so don't worry about that. Your other daughter (step-daughter) went to be with her mom. Your focus should be on the next step to make for when you do come home." Mom had spoken and with power and love in her tone, I snapped back just like that as I often did whenever she gave me the raw truth about life. So here I am with a bunch of strangers, women of all types, race and personality.

-----Trials and troubles may seem to overwhelm you but they cannot do more than work my will, this will not destroy me. Trust and go forward unafraid------

Day 2, I nearly fought a drug addicted woman over a blanket. I met a woman who was old enough to be my grandmother who had murdered her husband and was anticipating going home in a few years, The OG of the unit. Another woman walked around there like a zombie highly medicated it seemed, she had murdered her child by accident. I met a highly respected lesbian who gravitated to me and protected me so to speak, she kept me close and told everybody not to fuck with me, literally her exact words, after a while I was jailing. I didn't know if they were prolonging my stay wanting me to make a statement against my husband or what.

The charges were bogus and this was stretched to capacity. Although very uncomfortable, I knew that God must've had me there for a reason. I met a mighty woman of God whom I believed was one of Gods prophet. She was an abuser of drugs and had no place to call home but she ministered to my spirit like a good ole holy-ghost filled evangelist, God can and will use anyone. I was even able to build myself up and encourage some of the women. I read the bible with my jail mate & prayed with a few others. It was either the impact they had on me or me on them either way, God was in control and just maybe I needed to be there to pause for a moment and see where my life was headed to gain the mental strength that I needed for myself and my husband, after all he was in a bigger battle.

My mom kept asking me about commissary, they wanted to put money on my books so bad but I wasn't interested in no food or snacks. It took everything in me to make the decision to shower and I only showered twice in all the time that I was there. I had to wash my panties in the sink with my hands, ring them out and hang them to dry by a small vent. No privacy, squatting in front of strangers to take a dunk or piss and let's not discuss meals. It was plain nasty in there. Before I knew it 27 days had gone by and I was finally being released. The pants that I wore to jail were falling of my waistline by the time I got out. I had fasted for 27 days eating bread here and there and drinking water only but communing with the lord amongst a land that was unknown. Often times we're put in difficult situations, foreign environments. I knew whose child I was and that this was only temporary but just because this land belonged to others didn't exclude me from the path. I was finally released to my parents. I went to their home to shower and eat and it was just in time for me to pick my daughter up from school. She had been all these weeks without mommy and I wanted to be the first face that she saw when that school bell rang.

On my way to the Academy, I anxiously pulled into the parking lot lined up with the other vehicles. I parked waiting like all the other parents for our children to get out. I missed my daughter so much and I was so happy that I would be seeing her little face. The school bell rings and out walks all the little ones and there's mama's girl. I saw her coat before she could reach the exiting sign.

Our eyes met and I saw this huge smile on her face. I picked my baby up hugged her so tight "Hey Pooh, I missed you." She hardly reacted at all but that smile was good enough for me. I knew she was happy to see me, she was so smart and mature for her age that I was nervous about what she would even say but she didn't say much at all. She could be introverted at times. We went back to my parents after school and just relaxed for a bit before dinner and a movie. I had a new appreciation for the simpler things in life and I had a few hours of sanity until I had to start making phone calls, decisions & arrangements to see about my husband.

While I was waiting for pre-trial in a month, I was able to go visit my husband from behind a glass wall, at a jail that was even filthier than the one I had just left and to my surprise he was doing a lot better than I expected. We talked and laughed and talked some more. While I was in jail Rico's grandmother was handling a lot of the decisions concerning him. A lawyer was retained and we were already looking to go to trial. My husband was facing three charges Assault with intent to murder, premeditated murder and felony firearm. None of these charges were a walk in the park. This was a very scary moment for my family. This is when all the things that I prayed for, believed in sewed in faith for and cast down were put to the test. Would God show himself to be strong in this situation? Of course, My God is full of mercy and grace. It was never a matter of could God but would God and I thought why not. With God nothing is impossible and we are redeemed by the blood of the lamb.

-----Pour your mercy on my life-----

The day had come for me to go to court & I was fully convinced that my lawyer understood my position, especially as a wife and as a mother. Before going in to discuss the matters of my case, we spoke briefly and I told my lawyer as I've said many times before, I didn't feel as though I committed any crime and especially not the crimes in which they were trying to charge me with. Accessory after the fact of a felony is a felony charge and it states that I knowingly assisted someone after a crime had been committed. An offense punishable up to 5 years maximum in prison and/or fines and the charge for obstruction of Justice was another felony punishable up to a maximum of 2 years. I was looking at 7 years if I were to go to trial and lose. Each party spoke before the judge and prosecution did what prosecutors do best, they totally fabricated this story making me out to be this person that had no regard for authority or humanity. The character in which they spoke of was a stranger to me. My lawyer advised me to plead guilty and she would ask for the least amount of jail time. I kept telling her "No, I did nothing wrong, this was my husband, I only got emotional when I heard the officer threaten to blow his head off." "I did not interfere with their search nor did I assist him after a crime, this is my family," "yes, my mouth got a little too smart but that is all."

My lawyer looked at me and said "Do you want to go home today and be with your daughter?" I said "yes of course." She then said "well I'm going to be honest with you, this says the people vs Tyria Searcy so say for instance we plead not guilty and go to trial, Do you think that the juror would take your word over these officers." I said but I'm telling the truth, they should. "OK, I'm going to go even further as to say Tyria Look at you and look at them, you do not want to chance this." Without directly implementing race my lawyer was suggesting that I was just a young black girl against law enforcement, I won't win. I don't know if she wanted the conviction or what but for some reason I believed her and I was livid. "Tyria, Let me talk to prosecution and see what type of plea deal we can get you but think about what I've said, don't let pride keep you from your family." She said. I could not believe that after spending 27 days in jail. I am now choosing between what I believe is right and the common injustice of our sadly compromised system.

My lawyer came back and said that prosecutions offer was to drop the charge of accessory after the fact if I agree to one less than obstruction of justice which is a misdemeanor, no jail time just unreported probation for 10 years. I felt so low as if I was being backed in a corner. I felt wronged and totally taken advantage of. I had given them way too much already. I simply was not willing to compromise my truth, my integrity, my right to be heard. It would look as though they won. Call it pride or whatever you want but I call it reasonable for them to have dropped all charges, give me time served and let me tend to my husband.

This situation opened my eyes to another level of injustice and systemic racism without a doubt. I knew now that my husband was in big trouble, needless to say, I took the plea. With a racing heart, tears in my eyes and grinding teeth I took it, I took it for my family.

---Be selective with your battles sometimes peace is better than being right--- Tiny Buddha

Life Lesson 2 - when it rains, it pours!

It was at the hall of justice with a Judge on the 6th floor. This had been my place of permanent headache for the past several months. I saw the false evidence allowed in court for the jury to see, I've heard from coerced and threatened witnesses being manipulated into telling lies on down to misrepresentation from my husband's attorney. This entire trial was orchestrated in a strategic manner to frame a man with murder. Still surprised at the system & how clever it could be I somehow still believed that with his alibi and consistency, there was still a very good chance that Rico would walk free. The day came for the verdict after just a few hours of deliberation a jury of twelve gave their decision in the case against my husband. I paced the floor outside that courtroom praying and singing the words no weapon formed against me shall prosper, it won't work, only to go inside and hear GUILTY on all three charges. May 23, 2005 my husband was sentenced to Life without the possibility of Parole plus 15 years plus 2 years. How do you do get more than life? It was seeming like we needed to start this all over. I was in state of disbelief. I remember the feeling being similar to that of death. I had never prayed so hard and so much for someone's life, their purpose and their freedom. I felt as though God had let me down. I wanted answers that I had a hard time getting because I knew God was able and capable of doing just what I asked of him and it bothered me that he didn't. I don't know why but I took it as some sort of punishment. I felt I had been so authentic and pure hearted before the lord not spotless but I lived upright now and if I were to be honest it felt like a slap in the face as a believer. I went straight to my parent's house, ran up stairs, cut my phone off & I laid myself down on the couch and cried, I cried myself sick, I cried myself to sleep. I was literally mourning the fact that the man that I was in love with & had been married to for just 4 yrs. is no longer here with me. I didn't realize then how much of an impact this would have on my life but this day changed my life forever.

---Some things happen in our lives that have us questioning the God that we serve but father protect me from my ignorance and arrogance concerning your path for me & Direct me to your truth---

I was just getting use to companionship, my own family, my sanctuary and it was all taken away from me within a moment's time. I didn't realize how involved of a husband I had until he went away. I didn't even know my daughters clothes or shoe size because he took care of all of that. I was truly adapting to life without him. I knew we could file for an appeal but I had seen so many friends and family spend thousands of dollars and wait calendars before the courts would even consider granting them favor. Prayer was my only source and after a while even my prayers became few. I didn't know what else to do. Talking to my husband was satisfying at first and I would wait by the phone just to hear his voice on a daily basis, going to see him was the most frustrating process, I was not too pleased with officers or any authorities for that matter and to be searched thoroughly every visit was a constant feeling of humiliation. They always talk to you in an aggressive manner and to be monitored and told what to do and what not to do on visits was just as frustrating but at the same time my heart felt fulfilled because I got the chance to smell and hug him again. I had accumulated more fees than I expected with trying to help grandma with lawyer payments, keeping money on the phone and his books, letters and stamps, etc. a whole new world to adjust to but I was up for the challenge my hearts desire was to stick by my husband's side no matter what. I wrote letter after letter, made sure he got all the pictures he ever wanted, I sent monies, I visited often and then boom! We were denied our first appeal attempt. This put another dagger in my heart and I began to lose hope little by little but I was yet holding on. My daughter and I had moved back to my parent's home everything was totally different, my mindset was slowly beginning to change. Then the unthinkable happened July 20, 2006 my brother was murdered 6 days before his 33rd birthday, gunned down leaving a car wash on Hayes Street. His murder is still very painful to talk about, Mostly because I still remember the sound of my mother's cry so vividly in my mind but mainly because of all the rumors and accusations. Some people close to him to us may know more than their willing to say. We still haven't found the murderers. I had never witnessed nor experienced mourning in this way. Some coward hired a hit-man to murder my big brother. --O Lord God, to whom vengeance belongeth; O God, to whom vengeance belongeth, show thyself—Proverbs 94:1

Life was continuously happening and happening fast this was the biggest hurdle thus far. I couldn't believe that I was sitting front row of the church that I worshipped in starring at my brother's casket with him inside. I was heart-broken, confused, angry, and afraid. The two men that had taught me so much and protected me every step of the way were now gone, the two men that led my family in more ways than one. Although very different in their roles to me, they were both very similar in their actions towards family. My circle of love had an unrepairable hole in it. Life was no longer the same, the way I felt about life was no longer the same, the people in my life were impacted in such a way that they were no longer the same and people in general in life, I looked at them no longer the same. Again I looked to God in my discomfort.

I remember God saying to me that he had preserved my brother's life just so that he could get to know him better. My brother wasn't a believer of God and whatever it was that he was going through at the time, drew him to Christ because one day in that very same church that he was buried in, I watched my brother hold his hands up high in submission, in worship and it was then that he began to see clearer than ever before. God said to me that he could've died sooner but because he heard the prayers he allowed his acceptance first and although comforting, the pain somehow didn't lessen and the memories of my mother's pain couldn't be undone. I believed something changed within my brother's spirit and although how tragic and evil his exit from earth may have been, it must've been time but yet and still I hurt and I couldn't find encouragement anywhere not even in the church.

I began to drift away from my church family. I started going to church less and less and no one even noticed, so it was that much easier to stray away. Sundays became work days or days to relax despite how I really loved the lord. The hurt didn't separate me from Gods love but the things that were going on in my life were affecting me deeply. I had so many mixed emotions about what God was doing in my life. I had more time on my hands, idle time was the devil's tool to distract me. I began to live life unintentional again, just day to day living and trying to figure things out.

Ultimately, I had given the power to someone or something else other than God to help mold me into the person I was to be. I stopped communicating with God as much and in doing this I learned that I was being shaped into something that looked nothing like the person that I was called to be.

The world had its own plans for me but I thank God for prophet Jeremiah writings. For I know the plans I have for you," declares the LORD, "plans to prosper you and not to harm you, plans to give you hope and a future. I could have very well been on a road to no return but no matter where I found myself this scripture reminds me that if God be for me who could be against me because no one stands against the King. I could've finessed my way into a life that I felt I deserved but once you have the holy-spirit living on the inside of you. A lot of things that you long to do, you either cannot do or cannot get away with doing. I knew enough about God and yet I still found myself in a fallen state. I had fallen into a system that was never meant to handle my anointing.

My DNA was not about playing games and the enemy knew this about me. My brother was in and out of youth homes and prison since I was a young girl so that meant being in and out of my life yet he managed to teach me so much even in his absence because he always acted as the man of the house. I learned almost everything I know from what I know to be one the realist women alive, my mother. I was raised in the heart of the hood so I was never a soft individual at core. I was very knowledgeable as it relates to the streets. I was taught loyalty at a very young age & the people closest to me had credible resumes that solidified exactly where I stood as a person. I was never oblivious to the fact of how cold the streets could be. The streets always had the streets best interest in mind. The world has this crazy way of showing you love but not really loving nobody. However, I started to feed those habits that I thought had washed away but they began to resurface. If you are not careful the change that you now see in yourself is but a second away from the person you no longer wish to be. You're born with certain issues and your environment plays a part so in order to be totally free, it takes discipline and the constant intake of wisdom within your mind to replace the negative with that which is positive. I made an unconscious decision to keep going on to what was familiar to me because my vision had been blurred.

--Sin will take you farther than you want to go, keep you longer than you want to stay, and cost you more than you want to pay--R Zaccharias

    I started hanging out at the clubs meeting different people. After 6 years of dedication to God I knew how to be in the world even if I knew better. The real test was conquering how not to be of this world & that was the difficult lesson. It became impossible to keep my faith active and fluent because eventually what I seemed to be serving became God over me. In doing so, I became distant from my husband. I would still write him often but my number of visits went down. He knew there was a change in me but he was trying to keep focused on surviving in that dungeon and focusing on me just wouldn't make it any easier for him. Of course he noticed the shift in my life but he never said anything to me about it. I'm sure he had even heard from family members or friends that may have seen me out and about but still no mention of anything. When we talked it was about the girls, how he was doing, God & strength and ultimately about him coming home.

    We were both still focusing on the next steps in the process. Before I knew it about 2-3 years had gone by and I was starting to come up with all the excuses to give him, truth is I was searching, searching for answers, searching for fulfillment. I found rationalization in the fact that maybe, just maybe God didn't order me to suffer for a lifetime, doing a lifetime bid with Rico and in fact I believed that our relationship was outside of the will of God for me and the separation needed to happen. After all we became like night and day, unequally yoked. The fact that the judge hit the gavel and interrupted our plans didn't mean it was Gods plans for me. I felt bad in thinking this way, It would have been different for a fact had I known that he was coming home in say 10 years or whatever but he had no out date. Being that faith is sight beyond what I see it's safe to say that I lost faith in us after around the 3rd denial. I told myself plenty but the fact of the matter is I turned my back on the man that I vowed to stick by for better or worst. I tried so hard to be the best wife that I could be but I was disconnected and ashamed to even face my husband at this point.

That daily routine of church house wife that I was stuck in was no longer and finally I realized that there was life outside of being a parent & married. 26 years of age and I had approached a new stage of discovery. I learned me, what I liked, what I didn't like, what I had grown accustomed to and what changed about me. I believe everything happens for a reason and so if it be Gods will that Rico sit in prison for over a decade now and we separate as I walk paths alone and explore life as best I knew how then so be it.

Life Lesson 3 – Learn the roads that will lead you to nowhere..

I'm no rocket scientist but I know if you give too much attention to one thing, you're almost always neglecting another even if it's not deliberate. I was selfish in such a way that I started living my life outside of being a wife. I had no idea what that even looked like but as best I knew how for the moment, I decided to live. Although a little confused, I was somewhat single and sort of free, free to be me.

I was always close with my cousins. I had one more sibling left, we were only 15 months apart and closer than most sisters I know. My sister and I are so much alike morally and integral wise, we were just raised that way but we are also very different. I love the difference my sister makes. She has always offered me insight to a side of myself that I would have to stretch to tap into. It was just me, my sister & cousins. We all were in the discovery or exploring stages of life. We grew up with similar trials and things to overcome most of us so our bond was like glue. We stayed close to one another and we had each other's back, we fought together, laughed and cried together and we stayed connected. I had some really good friends but I had my family and that was my circle at the end of the day. We would all hang out, every weekend or every other weekend, often enough to know the same faces in the crowd at the club. Downtown was always a real good vibe. I mustn't forget about Club Envy nothing but family love there. I had my Birthday celebration there one stormy winter night in February and I felt like the whole city was celebrating with me, such a great turn out despite the weather. Having a good time was my new normal, enjoying life. In doing so it's inevitable that you meet people and develop new friends while just having a good ole time.

One night my cousin and I were just leaving a Bar and Grill, we were parked across the street at a Casino. We were waiting for valet to bring our car to us and there was this guy waiting for his vehicle as well. Me, being a people's person, it wasn't a big deal for me to start a conversation with someone or to say hello to a stranger. I love meeting new people, learning new things, cultures etc. I saw that he was very nice looking upon my first glance at him but what intrigued me the most was this distinctive jewelry he had on. He was wearing this chain with all these diamonds in it and it read 263.

I looked him in his eye and spoke to him and he spoke back, very polite he seemed or it could have just been the accent he seemed to have. He asked how was I doing, I answered "I'm fine, how are you?" I wasn't flirting at all, I promise not at the time although he was chocolate fine, groomed to excellence, smelled good, and nicely dressed but I just smiled. I said to him "that's a nice chain you have on, what does it stand for?" We're in Detroit and our area code here is 313 so I was interested in knowing the story behind 263 or where he was from. He said "Are you sure you don't know what this means," I said "NO, Is it where you're from?" and he said "yeah in a way." I was confused and I wanted to know more but our car pulled up. I was getting up from the bench to approach my vehicle and he said to me "before you leave, is it okay that I ask you for your number." I replied, "uh yeah, sure" and I gave him my number to call me. I was geeked, I wanted to continue our conversation anyhow. "I'm about to call you right now as soon as I get in my car so we can finish this" he said, and so he did.

He rang my phone and said "this is Ken, I didn't get your name" and I said "Tee, my name is Tee." He said "it was very nice talking to you for that short amount of time. I didn't want to let you go without getting to know you more". Smiling through the phone I said "well, I'm glad you asked because I felt the same way." I asked him where he was from and he told me that he was born and raised in New York and that he was here getting some things in order for himself because he had just gotten out of prison from serving a 5 year bid. I don't know what just getting out of prison looks like but it sure didn't look like him. I asked him again about the 263 on his chain and he said "you can look at your phone and the alphabets you see, that might tell you what you need to know." After hanging up the phone with him, my cousin and I both were looking at the phone at the numbers and the alphabets trying to make sense of it all and it dawned on my cousin almost immediately that the numbers probably stood for BMF. My cousin says to me "don't tell me this dude is a part of the Black Mafia Family." I had no idea who BMF was at the time, never had even heard of them.

I was totally clueless and based on my cousin's reaction I was unknowingly excited that I had met him too. My cousin told me, "Tee you have to keep talking to him, girl you never know what type of connections he could have." My cousin and I were kind of one in the same in a lot of ways. It seemed that she and I struggled the most out of all of us. We had more of a street mentality as well. She briefed me a little on their history as she knew it and from there I started to think okay well at least he might have a few dollars or something...Don't nobody want a broke man that don't know nothing. More so than money for some reason I was very attracted to street men, they reminded me of the men that I knew growing up that I was most comfortable with. I couldn't see myself with a man that was softer than me or one that didn't know anything about survival for one and loyalty first to be simply put, death before dishonor. I was raised with these values and the men around me from my uncles on down exemplified just that. Men that had the ability to protect you in more ways than one. I'm not saying that these kind of men only exist in the streets but there's something very different about a person being raised on love than one being raised on survival. I was raised on both so I was equally as different as a woman and I knew this about me. There was something about this guy Ken though that kept me calling his phone. Maybe it was the fact that this was the first man I took interest in since Rico had gone. I'm not sure but we ended our conversation that night with him saying that he would give me a call on tomorrow. I waited for that mans call and he never did. In fact he waited until the end of the week before he hit my line again and he didn't even call he sent me a text in the middle of the night that read "I'm thinking of you even when you're sleeping, I'll talk to you soon." That's what I woke up to in the morning and I must admit it made me blush. I assumed he had a lot going on and was a very busy person because that became a normal thing for him. He would often times text me very late at night saying things like "I'm thinking of you." It was as if he didn't have the time throughout the day but wanted to remind me by night that I was on his mind. We conversed on the phone but a few times, not too often it was mostly through text. Leave it up to me we would talk everyday but I didn't focus on that too much because we were just getting to know each other.

Finally we make arrangements for the two of us to see each other again. We agree to meet up at this condo that he said he had just rented out. He apologized in advance for the way that the condo would look inside because there was no furniture just a TV, a blow up mattress and some other items thrown here and there. I knew that he had just been released from prison so I didn't mind. In fact we chilled at this place for hours just talking about everything in life. In fact, whenever Ken and I would have a real conversation we would talk for hours on top of hours . We shared so many of the same interests. There were a lot of things that I didn't know about him because there were a lot of things that he just didn't want to share. I couldn't know too much too quickly about him it seemed and that just fueled me for some reason. Our entire getting to know each other process in the beginning turned into me trying to convince him that he could trust me enough to open up a little. I wanted to know more about him because I liked him a lot yet everything with Ken was cut and dry. He kept everything to a minimal; he discussed and shared with me the things he felt necessary for me to know at the time. We talked about his past as well as my past but I didn't want to share too much either considering. A lot of what he told me about his life and past was already public information regarding his family going to prison and them being under federal investigation and I felt it was all for his own gratification just to reminisce not to open up to me at all. Ken was a smart man, he reminded me of my husband in the way that he spoke with knowledge and intelligence. He was very strong in his statue as well, he could converse about anything at any given moment because he read a lot of books and self educated himself on many things. Everything Ken said made some kind of sense to me. I don't know if it was the Muslim background or what but his conduct was very attractive to me. I enjoyed his company and I always wanted him around. Ken and I started to hang out more and we became really good friends. After much thought I invited him to visit me at my apartment one night, it was really late because I had to be sure my daughter was asleep. I didn't want my daughter to see him or any man around me for that matter. It was way too soon and I never had a conversation with her about me and Rico possibly not being together but I'll never forget this night. Ken stayed the night and the next morning I got my daughter off to school without her knowing a thing. Ken woke up to pictures of my husband throughout my apartment in nice little frames about the wall and on the nightstand. Strangely enough he didn't say a word to me until he left the apartment and we talked on the phone later that night. I honestly didn't give the pictures a second thought. I never thought to flip them over or take them done after all it was my home and that was my heart displayed for everyone to see but obviously he began to think other thoughts like (there must be another man here with her.) This wasn't good for how secretive he already was. We started to talk more in detail about us, and how I wasn't so pleased with how on and off we were and basically asking him where we stood. It was then that he started to express to me how waking up to those photos made him feel especially not knowing what was really going on. I never discussed with him my most personal business because I was ashamed and he never really opened up to me either but I thought it would be a good idea to tell him about Rico and as we began to talk more, we discovered that we both had a somewhat similar past being that we both had just gotten out of a failed marriage, neither one of us divorced at this time but just separated from our partners that we both loved dearly. We stayed on the phone for hours again, while he drove the highway routes at night. That is where he could think most clearly on the freeway. Our conversation deepened that night and we realized that we both were on a risky path but we started to like each other even more. I respected Ken in the way that after learning of my husband and I, he empathized with our situation even though he had developed feelings for me. He never acted jealous of Rico. He would always ask me if I had talked to my husband, how he was doing and had I sent him monies lately, genuinely concerned. I can only assume he was this way because he had just come home from prison and he realized how important these things could be for a person incarcerated. Ken was a man of understanding for the most part but regardless of how he acted when it came to Rico, it was a totally different story when it came to any other man. He would always tell me that there was no room for another man in my life just him and Rico, nice of him to squeeze himself into the equation and maybe that's because he also knew that there was no other man in my life besides him and Rico and because Rico has life in prison he saw no real competition.

--Momma always told me to never open up one door without closing the other--

We both were interested in taking our love for each other to a greater level but at the same time we both were afraid, so much afraid that it was easy for years to have gone by before we even made things sort of official. One day Ken and I made a pack to focus on being together more often and with that meant we agreed to see each other three times out of the week no matter what. This way we progressed as a couple and to my surprise, he put forth the effort and kept his word, seeing me often.

It had been about 3 years of just dating, talking, sex and I didn't even know where the man that I loved laid his head at night. I was very much so exclusive with him. I had male friends but none of them got the time or attention from me that Ken did. He knew that my male friends were just around to pass time because he wasn't there and most of the times he wasn't there. This was quite an entanglement.

Ken was a Casanova, a charmer so to speak. He could win over many women with his charm, that's one of the reasons it was so easy for me to be okay with him touching bases with me when he quote on quote, could. Considering all that I was dealing with and my daughter not really knowing about him it worked out for us both actually but I got tired of that quick. The lack of commitment & communication was beginning to bother me and I was willing to take a leap. After all this time I still wasn't sure if it would be a leap of faith or a fall from grace but we began to grow together and move forward together. Our relationship got more interesting the more time we spent together. I still wasn't completely satisfied with the way that he moved and he wasn't too fond of the way that I was moving either especially when I would get together with my cousins. Ken would often tell me "Calm down Tee you out here in these streets and I'm hearing that you're here and there with this cousin and that cousin and I don't like it. I'm not just anybody, You can't just be out here hanging in the clubs and bars. You have to move differently because you're the closest person to my heart right now, you can't be everywhere easily accessible to everyone. Sit down somewhere and wait until I get off papers then we can move around, then things will be different." With Ken being on parole he was very antsy, strategic in his movement and he also walked on eggshells concerning the matters of his heart. He wanted me to do just what he said to do and it didn't matter if he didn't come around for the next month or so, I'd better be just where he left me, at home and being patient until he told me otherwise.

Everything was about him being on parole and this was the excuse he would use for things being the way that they were (temporarily) as he would say. I understood but only partially because the fact that I needed him to spend more time with me essentially would cost him nothing. We never went on dates, out to eat, to the mall, the beach, things that couples do. I was equally frustrated that I had to deal with his controlling mind games about what he expected of me and at the same time his lack of showing up. I became very independent upon my husband's absence and I wasn't feeling the fact that he wanted to control everything that I did yet ignore my sentiments.

I guess all the effort I put in for him to trust me, finally paid off. He finally revealed to me where he lived. Ken said he was tired of me thinking that he had something to hide. He was always very clear to me that there was no other woman in his life & no one else had his heart, only me. Ken came to the apartment one night and had me to follow his car with mines. He took me to this beautiful home that he lived in located in Farmington Hills. I couldn't believe he was opening up in this way. Finally I get to know where my man sleeps. I was beginning to feel like our situation was becoming a real relationship. I longed for that feeling again that pure connection between myself and someone that I loved. Even though he was opening up, Ken still played a lot of games. He would often come east to my apartment and because he now had a key he would stop by really late at night randomly. He would come in the house and before even speaking to me, he would go straight to the nightstand where I kept my phone and spend 45minutes to an hour investigating my calls, texts, accounts, etc. If he found something that he thought was weird, unexplainable or downright unacceptable he pitched a fit and that was his routine. Ken would either argue and fight with me about it or he would just leave and stay gone for weeks at a time.

It got to the point that I would be very cautious about what was in my phone even though I knew I wasn't with any other man. The smallest thing would tick him off. He wanted to see nothing that resembled male in my phone if you ask me. I wish I could ask the same of him regarding women but he would just tell me what I wanted to hear and continue on.

--Control is actually about power! Some may grow up not being taught how to embrace personal power in healthy ways--

There was this one guy that I was friends with and Ken didn't approve of it at all. He asked me to cut off all communication with him. I told him I would but the truth was, I didn't know how to end a friendship with someone that was a very good friend to me nothing more. This guy knew about Ken and I, we weren't intimate at all so I didn't deem it necessary to have that conversation of ending a platonic friendship with someone at the same time I felt obligated to honor his wishes so I did. I limited our talks and I cut off meeting up with him as well. I found myself making a lot of adjustments for the sake of our relationship and his Kens feelings. If he had even suspected that I was still talking to anyone or if guys were texting my phone, it gave this man all the reasons to act a fool, a justified fool in his eyes. Ken had studied 48 laws of power and had it down to a science if you ask me He would always use absence as a tool to gain respect or power over me. He controlled me through little acts of punishments. If ever things didn't go his way he would stay away for a while and for me that was torture because I didn't want to be apart from him not even for a day and especially for reasons that made me the blame.

---"When purpose is not known, abuse is inevitable"—Dr. Myles Munroe

While I spent much time trying to prove to Ken that I was faithful, he was dead stuck on thinking I was this sneaky individual. I don't know what gave him that impression about me but he would come sit outside my apartment in different vehicles a ½ block down the road or sometimes right out front, waiting to see if I ever were to have male company over at night. He never would, ever could witness that. I was honest with this man. Ken was the sneaky one, I couldn't help but think he was the one doing the cheating because he constantly made me feel like I was playing him in some way or another and that is what kept me at his mercy.

One night at about 2am in the morning, Ken and I are up watching a movie and a text from a friend comes through, in fact it was my bishop's son. He had texted me some obscene text out of the blue. I had no idea where that text came from, I had only talked to him a few times and I told him I was involved with someone and that I didn't feel comfortable with talking to him because of his parents but this night above all nights. Ken was right there waiting for me to pick up the phone. We were right in the same room. Ken asks "Who is it that texted you this late at night?" I said "Oh, that's this guy Tony from the church, just a friend" then he asked to see my phone. I don't even remember what was texted but Ken did not like what he saw. He felt that me and this guy had been messing around. I tried to plead with him even crying trying to convince him that I didn't know where that came from but Ken wasn't buying it. I don't blame him for not believing me. Out of all the things to text and out of all the hours of the day, how ironic. Ken was pissed, he went so far as to have me get naked and to the bathroom, "I think that you've been dirty so I need you to sit in this empty bath tub." He said. Ken told me that the only way he would stay and not leave and forgive me was if he could wash my sins away. I asked him what he meant by that and he went on to say that he needed to wash all my sins away and then he would forgive me. I said "okay" and sat in the tub naked as Ken pulled out his penis and urinated all over my naked body and that is what he considered washing my sins away "since, you wanna talk freaky with the pastors son" he said. Ken had a deep hate for the church because of how his grandmother raised him in it and as he called it slaved for the pastor.

He hated the church and always argued me about pastors being pimps and users. I'm not surprised that he came up with this "wash your sins away" for man to demonstrate making one clean again. I was even more surprised at myself for allowing that to happen but I was in love. Must've made him feel superior in some way but it certainly broke me down, the ultimate act of humiliation and control. I was slowly losing my self confidence. I remember the look on his face as he urinated as if it made him feel good. Imagine being completely innocent and still allowing this type of behavior that isn't even deserving for the guilty. Later on that day I talked to my friend who sent the text and he was very apologetic. He said that he had been drinking and didn't mean to send that text to me but what was done was done, it didn't matter. I certainly didn't feel the need to discuss with him the aftermath of that. I was willing to do anything possible to keep my man around and that was the bottom line. That's why I let him do what he did. I had been groomed into the weakest version of myself, a person that I had never met before. The things I would do and allow was to simply assure him that he was the only man for me and he used my weakness for him as bait.

He broke me down on plenty of days and most nights. The majority of our relationship I was actually sad & alone more than I was with him but I was fighting for him to be there even if it meant I wasn't all the way there. I'm not sure if I had become afraid for another man to leave me like my husband did but it was pathetic as a woman.

Ken was always away in the streets claiming to be handling this business and that business but barely presenting the fruits of his labor. Every time I thought I had a grip on life, life showed me I didn't. This is when I became more and more unrecognizable. Tyria had become consumed with Ken thoughts about me and proving to Ken my worth as he should see it, I was completely lost!

--Whatever you are willing to put up with, is exactly what you will have—

Life Lesson 4 - *No need to put up a fight*

Things with Ken and I became a little more complicated when he somehow convinced me to move west closer to him out in Farmington. He said he would help me out with anything that I needed and I wouldn't have to worry about much of anything. Ken always talked to me with such a confidence that made me believe in him. No matter what he did I believed two things, that he loved me above any other woman and that he was going to always make sure that I was straight. How did I believe these things when he never showed me in action simply because he told me. Ken took his time with my heart and my mind, he was master of manipulation. I believed he spoke from his heart but things never panned out the way he intended them to. I never wanted to believe he fed me lie after lie for some reason. I wasn't the female to want or ask him for his money or for much of anything for that matter. I always believed if a man be a real man and he's with a woman. He will see that there is a need and he will meet it. Without her having to ask him to, as a man you do the obvious. Ken had a different perspective, he always saw me working and making things happen on my own so I guess he assumed that I didn't need help from him but I did. I guess the old rule applies, closed mouths don't get fed.

Ken had all kind of money and this is true because I saw it with my two eyes. I would hold on to his money for him thousands of dollars at a time. Based on what my eyes saw, he never took care of me like I knew he could have but I never got that deep into his business when it came to that. I didn't even know how he made a living I just knew he wasn't your 9-5 worker because of the lifestyle he always presented before me. The most I've had in my possession of his at a time was around $70,000. I had his money locked away in a safe at my bank and only my hand print had access to it. He would often times instruct me to do little things that benefited him so trust was no longer an issue. All the while I could be low on groceries but he knew the type of person I was. I never stressed him about money, I paid my own way even if I got behind on bills, my problems were my problems and I hated that about him because he would turn the blind eye to my problems but he loved that about me that I would work to solve it all on my own. Ken would tell me "There's a time to be noticed and a time to lay low".

    I became quite uneasy in our relationship with trying to keep up with who he wanted me to be but he was never really honest to me about who he was, a lot of things I had to figure out on my own. In figuring things out, I would pop up at his place or condo in the wee hours of the night just to see what he was doing. I've even caught different women there with him at times. Ken hid who he really was and created this image of himself that he wanted me to believe him to be. It frustrated him that his true self was unveiling to me little by little. One night I called his phone several times and he didn't answer so by morning I decided to drive by his place to see what was up. I saw his car parked in the lot of his condo so I knew he was there. He had just been ignoring my calls per usual or he was there with someone. I never needed to be buzzed in for entry. I would just wait on one of his neighbors to approach the door and walk in right behind them. They saw me there all the time so no one found it strange, his neighbors would just let me right on in.

    I walked up to his door, knocked twice and some light skinned female with long wavy hair and a funny shaped nose opens the door to greet me. She stood in the doorway of his condo wearing his t-shirt asking me who I was there for. I asked "Where is Ken?" She had this look of confusion on her face. Ken comes rushing to the door after hearing my voice asking me what I was doing there, as if he didn't realize he had been ignoring my calls all night. The better question is "why, is she here this early in the morning Ken?" but it was obvious, she had stayed the night, she had on my mans t-shirt with nothing else. Ken was so mad at me that we began to tussle at the door because he didn't want me to get inside, in the midst of the struggle I was thrown to the ground and he literally dragged me down three flights of stairs as I kicked and fought him. He had my feet and my arms so it was difficult for me to defend myself. We fought for about an hour and a half long. He was trying to get me to leave first so he could have this girl get in her car to leave. The girl seemed afraid that I would attack her but I wasn't going to attack her at all, I mean unless she said or did anything to change that. I was loud and I said some really mean things but my issue was with him and at this point he really pissed me off fighting me. Ken had never put his hands on me before.

He was emotionally treacherous yes but besides our bathroom incident, he had never really gotten physical with me. This day he bust my lip and sprang my ankle from dragging me, I had to get crutches. Ken's neighbor came out from hearing all the commotion and yelled at him not to put his hands on me again. Ken told him to mind his business before a bigger problem occurred and the neighbor stood alongside his balcony quietly watching as if to make sure Ken didn't hit me again and he didn't.

Ken begged me to let this girl leave in peace. She waited until he gave her the ok and she left. I let her walk to her car, get in and pull off in peace. He began to apologize for putting his hands on me and busting my lip after seeing that the blood continued to flow, he felt so bad this was our first physical altercation. He said he didn't know what else to do but to get physical with me because he didn't know what I was capable of. After this fighting for us became our new normal in a way. I don't know why Ken was so mad at me for coming over uninvited he knew I hated to be ignored and besides he popped up on me all the time unannounced and I always would pop up at his. Difference is I was faithful, he was not. There was never an issue unless he was caught doing something shady.

Ken said that this girl was just somebody he had met and was about to do some business with her and her family. She didn't even know his name was Ken. He had given her some other name which explained the confusion on her face when I asked where Ken was. He turned this completely around making it my fault for putting his name out there to someone that he supposedly wasn't trying to get to know like that "typical Ken" to now be so angry at me for being "typical me" Strikes me as odd that it was strictly for business because I'm about 99 percent sure that he slept with that girl that night but of course he would never admit to that. It was just me again interfering with his money. "I can't work with you around Tee" he would always tell me. There were other times that I would go to his condo with a blanket and overnight bag already in hand even though I was uninvited. I waited on him to arrive so I could go in and we can talk.

He got so use to me stopping by unannounced that one night when I fell asleep outside in my car waiting on him to arrive, he pulled up and knocked on my car window to awake me and said just come on inside Tee.

Our relationship was a little different and it was in severe trouble because we dealt with so many insecurities within ourselves and trust issues and the abuse was so deep on a verbal, emotional and now physical level that we were clearly on a rollercoaster. When things got physical we had become even the more toxic to one another. We let our emotions out all kinds of ways that were unhealthy to any relationship.

-A man without self-control is like a city broken into and left without walls.-Proverbs 25:28 esv

There was a clear mental breakdown that took place and emotionally I wasn't the same, there was a disconnection between me and my highest self. If ever you want to know why you feel broken know that it doesn't happen overnight. In order to break someone down you have to first work on their mind. The ridiculing, rejection, silent treatment, screaming and rage that Ken and I displayed toward one another was shameful. We wanted to be heard and to have our own way. I realized it started with the way he molded me. I tried to fight back and gain back pieces of me that I knew I had lost. We lacked so much but yet we yearned for a certain power within the two of us. We were both two strong minded individuals and after a while, we clashed simply because of our strength.

Ken had so many controlling ways that once he got inside of my head, he was pretty much able to do anything he wanted to do and I would let him. Everything was gradual, it increased ever so slowly. He never wanted me to catch on to his shenanigans. He needed me to be accustomed to the way he treated me as a part of our normal daily routine and not say a word so I normalized it. I realized that Ken needed to be secretive towards me in order to use other women to get things accomplished that he wanted. That's why I became a big problem for him & his business deals were hindered. It kept him from making money and making the moves that he wanted to. At least that's what he always told me.

I always grew to believe that no matter what you're doing on the streets and no matter whom you're doing it with. No one should come before your lady. You never let home feel the wrath of your lack of ability to be disciplined and make sound decisions. You protect yours at all costs and if this type of respect is felt, peace at home is inevitable. Besides Ken had money that I never got a chance to fully enjoy and then on top of the disappearing acts. I was so confused.

It was the weekend of July 16th, my sister's birthday celebration we had a good ole time in the club swaggin' and surfin' and popping bottles in our booth all night long until the lights came on. As we prepared to leave the club, a huge fight outside the club breaks out and I'm in it. Me, this chick, her friend and my cousin were the first to brawl out. My sister & a few other cousins who were just a few feet away saw us and noticed us fighting so they jumped right on in because that's what we do. Here's how this all went down.

There was this chick that had come up to Ken in the club and said that someone had just tried to steal his car from valet and Nisha had to let valet know that, it wasn't this guys car to prevent this dude from driving off in Kens car. Ken ran outside and I ran out behind him and there this Nisha girl was. Now whether she was running goods or money for Ken I don't know. I just know when we got outside she was getting out of the driver's seat asking Ken to help her to park his car, expressing that she had just saved it from someone who was trying to ride off in it. She obviously knew his car very well to identify it amongst others but not well enough to know you push to park a BMW. As she's getting out of the driver's seat to allow him to park I can't help but notice this smirk on her face. It must've been the expression on my face but she turns to me and says hello then turns to Ken when I didn't respond and says to him, who is this chick?

Her friend then got upset & says my friend said hello as to force me to speak to her friend whom I didn't even know but then as she saying this she hits me on the top of my head with a promotional flyer that she had in her hand. It was a light pop on the side of my head as if I was a kid and it was oh so disrespectful before I could swing on her, my cousin did. She swung on the friend first and next thing I know it was going down in the middle of the street outside a club in downtown Detroit. Jewelry was lost and broken, Ken grabbed me up in the air by my waist mid fight as I'm kicking and fighting to be let down. He totally took me away from the altercation but also made me vulnerable to be attacked so I was crazy mad. My family had gotten upset because they are now involved and fighting some girls and they don't even know why. If this isn't crazy enough, we had some male family members there as well and they started to pull out their straps, they had popped the trunk and everything, it was so chaotic. No one knew what could possibly happen and It was unclear to them who was all involved. They didn't know if Ken was with me or what other guys were involved so they were just getting ready. It was bananas but I immediately stepped in and let it be known that Ken was with me and everything was good but what did Ken do. He got in his car and pulled off in anger as if he had just been disrespected.

    It's safe to say the flyer popper had one too many drinks that night and furthermore she had no idea that I had so many people with me. When Ken pulled off I began to call his phone as I'm driving away wanting to clarify with him what in the hell had just happened and he's telling me that I let a dude pull a gun out on him, typical Ken stuff. If any little leap hole to point the finger in another direction than at him he will be all over the opportunity, when in fact I kept him from getting seriously hurt that night considering none of my male friends or family members had ever met him. However what do I do but cater to his emotions per usual so I'm trying to explain to him everybody's position and what really happened but he wasn't listening. I decide to detour from going home and I tell him, I'll meet you at the condo and he agreed but then he stopped answering his phone once I got closer to his home. Ken wasn't heading to the condo he was on his way to the hospital to accompany these chicks we just fought who felt they needed some medical attention. We find that miss drunk friend, arm had gotten broken during the fight and she was in a lot of pain and had to stop at a nearby emergency room.

    I didn't care nor was I sorry my concern was "why is my man there with them and not here with me?" I waited in his parking garage. He got to the house a couple hours later saying that his phone had no reception and he had been at the hospital and of course it was all my fault that I messed up "business" again.

"She did a lot of running for me," he went on to say "We made a lot of money together." He said he had to go make sure that they were ok to make sure his connect was still good. This man had a story for the books every time and yes I believed him of course I found out otherwise but I believed mostly everything this man would say. If there was a picture of a fool in love, it would show me. I knew that there could have been partial truth to what he was saying but still taking into consideration the lies. I would bet my last dollar that he was manipulating these women into believing something different about him just as he did me and that he was sleeping with the so called help or runner for that matter. He was a womanizer, if ever he was doing business with a woman it was for his gain in more ways than one. I couldn't get pass the fact that in that moment he made a decision that made him look more loyal to them than me in front of my entire family.

    We argued and argued that night and then we went inside and made love and woke up the next day and pushed it all under the rug like nothing had occurred at all or at least until we felt like mentioning it again. This is how unhealthy and conditioned we both had become but this time the fight was different. This particular incident left a stain on me because out of all the talks that we had for hours upon hours about trust and loyalty and how much we meant to one another I felt betrayed by his actions. Ken and I had lost contact once again, he was so frustrated he disappeared but then he popped back up in my life again. This time I had started to move on for the first time. It was the longest he had been away. It had been about 4 months. I was hurt by him one too many times. I started talking to someone else and he had obviously heard about it. Ken comes back around to be nosey and here we are again. I would drop everything and everybody because Ken is back and he's the one and only. Me trying to date someone while he was around never worked. He knew what he was doing and of course every issue that we tried to bury would eventually rise again. I believe Ken was shocked that I was actually attempting to move on from him and besides the guy that I started dating wasn't no bum out here either. His name held just as much weight so it could've been an ego thing however he knew that all that back and forth. Years of on and off was getting old and I was ready to experience something better.

More so than that, Ken was in a rut and needed some place to go is how I looked at it because although he never said it, He just started coming back around and after so many times of staying the night and leaving this article of clothing and that piece of jewelry, couple pairs of shoes, he was sort of moved in. I'm not sure what got a hold of him on the streets but he seemed to be more humbled and really trying to make our relationship work this time but he just kept bringing up this guy that I started dating and I kept bringing up these women that he was with throughout the entire 4 ½ years of us being together. I could tell that Ken had started to make an effort in disconnected with his female companions. He was at home mostly and we were working on a better commitment. Yes there was still a couple of females hanging on and one stripper that I couldn't stand with texts in the middle of the night and random calls, I can honestly say he was weeding them out. He would sometimes leave in the morning and stay out until about 4am the next morning or sometimes not even coming home but he wasn't contributing to any bills, so now this is a problem. I could obviously tell he wasn't getting money like he was but now I felt like he was using me for a place to stay. I was really the only woman he could trust.

I didn't trust him at all though and we tried to be a better couple but we were like two political competitors the way we argued our points and views and the way we fought in the house like two WWF contenders it was horrid. Ken even knew just where to hit me so that I wouldn't bruise. He would hit me on the top of my head or some other random place on my body as if he had been doing this all his life. He would demonstrate to me how to hold my head when laying down after a fight to avoid my eye from turning black and blue because all the pressure would go to one side of my face that I was lying on. I was a fighter but I never fought so much in a relationship, my husband and I even had our moments but this was exhausting. We tore that place up at times there wasn't a such thing as just hitting on me. I hit his ass right back, kicking, punching, fighting, biting, scratching whatever it would take.

I absolutely am a defender of myself by nature. I fought throughout school defending myself so I definitely fought back and sometimes I hit first depending on how hurt I was. I was one that defended myself against verbal attacks as well and I'm sure my mouth got me into a lot of unnecessary fights with him but there was no shutting me up. He often compared my mouth to that of AK47 he said some things that I would say were like a shot gun and it hit him hard. Me being very passionate about love and the way I wanted love to feel. If ever I felt like I was losing control of that feeling I would make some noise just to make my presence none. I would openly let it be known when my feelings were hurt and I would demand him to fix it right away. The toxicities worsened.

--A deep need for unhealthy love masks a very fragile self-esteem and troubled relationship--

He would leave and I would call this man's phone at least 30x a day, miserable in bed dialing him back to back to back. I would leave voice messages crying and pleading for him to call me or text back. One time he left and I thought he was gone for good because he took all his clothes with him not leaving a single item in the closet. I called him crying on his voicemail that I was going to take a whole bottle of pills and take my life in hopes that he would come by and check on me but he didn't answer, he didn't show up, I heard nothing from him at all, I was low.

I didn't even know where all of this was coming from but I was desperate for a man that brought me mostly pain. I had to quit a couple of jobs because of the physical bruising I incurred. I had just got hired at Q Loans, through a third party company, I prayed for this job. I was so excited to be in this position even though it was entry level I understood how I could advance within the company being a quick learner and I was so excited. I left one day after work I got into a huge fight with Ken at home over God knows what and instead of taking that walk of shame to my cubical with a black eye the next morning, I never went back. Ken was some character and I was too. Things got a little bad with his money flow and he became stressed. I tried to be there for him to encourage him. I cooked him hot meals, I rented him vehicles to go out and try and get his money back together. I even loaned him money for him to flip and I never got a red cent back.

Ken had more excuses than most. I didn't know what was going on with him in the streets honestly, I just knew that he always made promises that he didn't keep. I fell behind in bills trying to help him get back up on his feet and I finally said to him I need for you to help me come up with this amount of money by this time or else were going to be evicted, rent had fallen behind and he couldn't deliver. We argued fussed and fight up until the day we were put out and even after.

Had it not been for the court order and me losing my apartment, I probably would have never left Ken but we were separated this time and this time I felt it was for good. Kens mom and I had developed a good relationship and I would still go visit his moms often and even she would tell me that Ken wasn't acting the same as of lately. Every time we talked he would promise that I would only be at my mom and dad's temporarily, that he was coming back for me and Shy whom he had grown to care for and love. Deep down I knew that this was just like any other promise he had ever made, empty. I knew that with us being a part it allowed me to look back at our relationship and all the things that he had put me through, that we put each other through and make a sound decision concerning us. The person that I had become chasing after him and what I thought we had, was totally dark and I was able to view us from a different angle. I realized just how unhealthy we were for each other.

It was a relief to my daughter that we had to leave, I'm sure. She didn't appreciate our fighting one bit although he would never hit me in front of her, she only caught us fighting once but the arguing was non-stop. There's no hiding unhappiness from a child no matter how hard one tries. Your child is connected to you like no other. Ken did his best to be the best he could be for the both of us based on who he was at that time in his life and my responses, well I did the best I could in responding to. The behaviors were my patterns.

My daughter and I are back living at my parent's and it's officially my daughters 10th grade year in high school she had to move away from all her friends and come back east to attend a school that had a gun shooting outside in the parking lot on her very first day. This was validation that things would get interesting. I felt really bad but it is what it is. We were making the best of our current situation. No more Ken, the phone calls lessened and he eventually did what he does best and that was disappear this time is was out of town. He went on to continue his journey in Arizona. I was blessed to still have my position as a medication distributer at an assisted living facility still making decent amount of money that would allow me and my daughter to get back on track quickly and as for my heart well it was scattered on the side of the road in a million pieces and left for me to pick up. I made a vow never to allow a man to bring me so low again and I meant this whole heartedly.

—There are costs of pleasure and benefits of pain, learn of the two---

Life Lesson 5 – Dear Charles

It was a Friday morning, I worked my 4 hours for the day and I was exhausted from my previous 12 hour shifts so you can only imagine how fast I aimed towards the door before I heard any urgent need for the nursing staff. I rushed to my car and was so excited to see the sun beaming through the clouds in spite of the brisk winds that followed. It was finally the weekend and I had a lot on my mind. I was ready to finally relax but I was going nowhere fast because as soon as I got in my car to start it, I was reminded that I was low on gas. The tank was beyond empty. I immediately headed towards northwestern highway to the nearest gas station, normally I would've taken my chances on empty, that's just how much I despised stopping for gas.

I made it, pulled in to the gas station & opened my car door when I noticed some papers that I should clean out from my drivers inside door. With one foot out of the car I noticed this guy sort of staring at me as he walked inside the gas station. I kept cleaning and eventually got out to trash the items and to go inside for gas. Walking in the station, the first aisle to my left was this same guy accompanied by a young boy. I walked passed them and went on to grab my usual; a candy bar, a juice and potato chips. Standing in line to pay for gas as well, this guy stepped up behind me almost interrupting me talking to the attendant and he's asking me if I am married? As I repeated $20 on pump 5. I hesitantly turned to him and said "NO". I heard him mumbling something else but I walked out of the gas station not wanting to be bothered.

As I'm pumping my gas he pulled his car around to the side where I was and rolled down his window asking if he could get my number to call me sometimes, something inside of me said to just keep going and say no. I replied and said "Uh, I don't know, I really don't need to talk to anyone right now." He said "me either, I just want to be your friend nothing more...You're so beautiful I had to say something." I didn't know what to say I usually don't know how to let someone down. "What's your name first off," and he replies "Chuck and yours?" "Tyria, thank you and nice to meet you Chuck now what were you saying, Chuck" He asked for my number again and I reluctantly spoke aloud my cell phone number, as I'm telling him he's dialing me from his phone. He asked where was my phone, letting me know that he was dialing me right away and to store his number in my contacts. I could hear my phone vibrating from inside my car. "I will lock you in Chuck" he replied "okay bet" and got in his car to leave.

--Its always good to follow your first mind---

I got in my car and headed towards the freeway to my parents, I began to think "Why did I give him my number..well, maybe he's different. You should be open to meeting new people. He was very well dressed and smelled really good, why not?" Reflecting back on my last relationship and how things went all wrong. All that I could say was, Thank you God for another day at trying to get things right. Just maybe.

After about a half hour of driving on the highway and thinking to myself, I am home sweet home. Home has always been where mom and dad lives. I love the fact that their doors are always open to me when I need them to be and even when I lived away this was my home away from home. It's my safe haven, my comfortable place.

I had very little time to relax before I had to head back out to pick my daughter up from school. After picking her up I finally get back home to kick my feet up & who do I get a call from but Chuck from the gas station. I wasn't doing anything, I was chilling so I answered & we must've stayed on the phone at least two hours that day. We talked about a little bit of everything. Oddly enough we really connected in conversation. I was surprised at how open he was with me in our very first conversation but he said to me, "I have nothing to hide My name is Charles O'Neil born February 4th and I just got out of prison, I served 5 years and it's been about two years since I've been home" Ok, whoa that was a lot I expressed, I asked him "What did you go to prison for?" he told me it was a long story but I could look him up if I wanted to, it was nothing too bad. He expressed how happy he was to be out of prison because he hated being in there and went on to say that he would never go back. "I would love to take you out on a date?" He says telling me how beautiful he thought I was when he saw me. He said his initial thought was "She look like she know something, she has to be somebody's wife" I chuckled in a blushing manner and replied "but I had on scrubs coming from work" and he said "yes and I can only imagine how good you look outside of your work clothes." I giggled even more at his many compliments. It sure felt good to be complimented. Ken never did that. I wasn't one to reveal much about my personal life upon meeting someone but I did tell Charles that I had some things going on with me that I would explain later.

I was still quite weary to develop anything with anyone so soon, Ken and I had just broken up and on the surface here is another man just coming home from prison, It seemed as though I couldn't escape the ex cons.

Chuck asked me if I noticed that he walked with a limp, I said "no, I sure didn't." He said "yeah, one day a guy tried to rob me, He ran up on the side of my vehicle one night as I pulled in the driveway to get out of my car. He put a gun to my head demanding that he walk me in the house so he could get what was inside, money or whatever." Charles went on to say that because he didn't show any signs of being shook or nervous and remained very calm that it made the guy even angrier that he wasn't willing to comply. Charles said His initial thought was to fight back and get this gun away from him so he went for the gun and began to tussle with this guy over it. Things were getting tough and it wasn't as easy as he thought so he said he just took off running in hopes that he could get away but He said the guy pointed the gun at him while he was running away and started shooting and shooting... Charles said "He shot him like 6,7 times until he fell to the ground, he then came and stood over him as he laid on the sidewalk. Charles said all he could think about in that moment was his son and he even said to the guy "Man please, I have a little boy" Praying that he wouldn't kill him but that wasn't enough because he pulled the trigger again and again close range and shot him a few more times to finish him off. The guy ran off with no money or valuables but one's life was on the line. Thank God that somehow help was on the way and he was taken away by ambulance where he survived and was treated.

"Oh my God" I replied (in total shock) "that's terrible that someone would do that to you" He told me that he hasn't been the same since that day this happened to him, physically or emotionally and that he was lucky to still be alive and I reminded him it was more than luck I would say you're blessed. He goes "yeah, I know I'm blessed it's just that sometimes it's still so hard for me. It was hard for me being in the hospital trying to recover with very little help from my family." Charles said that his family wasn't there for him like he thought they should've been and he believed it was because they were afraid to be around him. However after rehabilitation and many blessings from God he's still here. "Often times I get really angry about my situation but most times I'm so grateful. I just pray and hope that one day things will get better." I agreed with him and encouraged him to keep strong because one day things would have to get better.

    We continued to talk about our personal interest, our past pains and our future wishes. We shared most of the same wants and desires. Charles asked if I was in a relationship with anyone and I told him no, explaining that I had just ended an on again off again relationship that I was involved in for about 5 years. I wasn't completely over him so soon but I was definitely tired of the back and forth.

I moved back in with my mom and dad after our break up and since then I've been striving to move forward with my life. I knew that our relationship was difficult to understand so I didn't dare try to explain it to anyone. I didn't tell Charles I was married either because I wasn't sure if we would go any further than our first date but after talking to him on the phone almost every night I knew I had to tell him because I was beginning to like him.

    I never mentioned my husband to anyone unless I felt I was growing closer to them. My husband was still very present in my life and there could be no hiding that fact. In fact Rico advised me never to tell him about any other guy that I was dating. He simply didn't want to hear about it and so I didn't. He moved on as well, yes even in prison. He started to build meaningful relationships with women and that's how it was between us. We were cordial and we were cool but I was still out here figuring things out. I told Charles my last relationship was an experience that I never wanted to revisit again. The pain, mental anguish and just the overall way that I felt being with him was disheartening. I told him about the promises Ken made to never cheat again, to never to hit me again, never to degrade me again, never to misuse me again. I believed all the lies for years and years until one day, I finally woke up. There were so many warning signs I had to leave that relationship. It could've been the countless number of females, the car repossession, eviction, lost of wages but whatever it was, I finally woke up. I couldn't give him every detail but I wanted Charles to understand the emotional damage I had just experienced and how it opened my eyes to the person I was becoming and how I never wanted to put myself in that position ever again.

    Charles listened on and he said to me, can I ask you a question, "why was it that he would hit you at times?" I told him, "Ken would always say it was my mouth! He used his hands to shut me up at times he found it disrespectful for me to get nasty with him in words and although I agreed, I was only mouthy when I tried to defend myself. I knew my words could bruise him good."

    Charles went on to say "yeah that mouth will get a woman in some serious trouble, laughing on he said that's one thing I will not tolerate and that's disrespect from a woman" I paused for a moment and took in his reply and I said to him "my mouths not that bad and if it was I had my reasons." It was the only weapon I had to defend myself. I knew I couldn't beat him physically so I used words to sometimes fight for me.

    I say lots of things that I don't mean in the midst of a heated argument but I was tired of fighting in more ways than one. Chuck listened and agreed but again he stated "you women need to learn that every man is not having that talking back stuff." I let it go without addressing it the next time, I know what type of woman I am and I knew the type of love that I would freely give and all I wanted was respect and genuine love in return. We were just beginning to know each other. I was confident that he would understand later on. Besides Ken and I situation was so complex only a few would understand. "Speaking of past relationships, exes and damage being done, I have some past hurts of my own," Charles said.

    He went on to tell me how he is single but he lives with a woman currently. "Wait a minute so like right now, you live with a woman?" Yes, he said, "We were together at one point but she's no longer my girlfriend, we are just living in the same household until I get back on my feet." He said, it's been very difficult for him to make certain moves like he wanted to because the streets were not like they used to be when he left 5 years ago therefore he's been there with her for longer than he expected but assuring me that soon he'd be away from her all together. Charles said this woman that he lived with was fully aware that they were not together and asked me not to read too much into it for me not to think otherwise. He went on to say that while things weren't going so great for him mentally nor money wise she stepped out on him and had sex with the father of her child something she promised that she would never do. She had a daughter previously by another man and he said that they set some ground rules regarding her relationship with the father of her child & in particularly regarding her being with him again, agreeing that this was something that she would never allow to happen. He appeared to be a little insecure about the entire thing.

 Charles said he knew her daughters father (they were friends at one point in time) he said he was like an OG to him and taught him a lot about the streets coming up but then when Charles went away to prison, he started to date her knowing that she has always been the girl that chuck would connect with from time to time. Chuck felt betrayed by the both of their actions and it was something he didn't get over. Although she begged him for his forgiveness, he said he could never forgive her.

 I asked him "Why is it so hard for you to forgive her and if he thought that could possibly reconcile things? I mean she seemed like a nice girl to be holding things down at home while you get back on your feet." He told me that she was a really nice person and she was his really good friend more than anything. She just made a lot of dumb decisions he said and most were influenced by her family and friends.

 Charles said he had known her since her early teenage years and they talked on and off for years. He looked out for her plenty of times when he had money so she was no stranger to the type of man that he was. He told me that he loves her but every time he tried to get over what she did to him, he couldn't. "It hurts me to even look in her eyes, I couldn't believe that she would do that to me. She still wants to make things work and wants us to be together again but that was the point of no return for me so as soon as I get myself back on track, I'm leaving and she knows it."

My intuition as a woman kicked in and I thought to myself "You're there because you want to be there" I clearly had trust issues but I could hear some truth as he further explained his pain. I had to believe what he said at least until I found out otherwise. I wanted to give him a fair shot. He had been so open and brutally honest with me thus far. I couldn't have asked for more sincerity.

We continued to talk, I told him about my daughter, and how great of a relationship we had and how proud of her I was, always doing well in school academically, very respectful kid and for having a good head on her shoulders. I was proud to have raised a young lady such as herself. He told me about his children, a boy (14) and a baby girl (1). He got married while he was incarcerated and came home to the woman he made his wife ready to build their marriage & family but the money was low and things were different.

He said his wife couldn't stand the rain long enough so she packed up and left with their daughter. They are now separated and she gave him the hardest time whenever he would ask about seeing his daughter. Charles missed his baby girl so much. I could hear the brokenness all in his voice whenever he spoke of her. His wife moved 3-4 hours away to Ohio. Charles motivated her enough to get back in school to get her GED and she went on to a Nursing Program in Ohio to pursue nursing afterwards. It was extremely hard for Chuck knowing he couldn't go be with his daughter when he wanted to. I would just listen to him and try to process it all. I didn't want to judge his current situation especially knowing I had some issues of my own but I asked him, how well is your relationship with your son? He told me that it was going good, they were just getting back on track since he's been home from prison. Charles raised his son from an infant child all by himself. He was in a much better financial situation than the mother so he didn't hesitate to take care of him full on while his mom got things in order and besides that he sort of didn't have a choice because one day she dropped their baby off to him and never came back to get him. Chuck fed, clothed, raised and taught his baby boy from a young age everything he needed to know but then when he went away to prison and he had to go back to his mother. Now that Chuck was back home, He wanted nothing more than to fall right back on track with his son. Charles said things were a little different now because his son had gotten older and he has to undo a lot of his bad habits that he learned while he was away. "My son was with me when I met you," he said. "Oh okay, yeah I do remember seeing a young guy with you at the gas station." I replied.

We continued to talk about everything you could think of…after hours and days of talking everyday becoming more & more acquainted, I must admit I had mixed feelings. Charles had a lot going on too, in fact it seemed like much more than I was prepared to deal with. He was married with a new baby and obviously not with his wife because he's living with another woman so that alone required an exhale. I thought to run as fast as one can but I felt more empathy for Chuck than anything I wanted to offer him a genuine friendship and more understanding to help him navigate through his feelings. Charles was very sad at times and it showed. It had only been a week or so and I felt like I knew so much about him already. Our first date hadn't even been planned yet.

We decided to hook up for a date and since he lived deep west and me further east, we decided to meet each other halfway at another gas station. This guy and I had a thing for gas stations. Once we met up, I followed him to his friends house and it was there that I parked my car to get in with him to begin our date. We had no real plans we just went out quickly to grab something to eat and then we went by this bar that was owned by one of his close friends.

We hung out there at the bar for a while, had a few drinks and talked a bit. Charles and I both had been through a great deal of pain in our past relationships and the bruises were still fresh but we attempted to trust one another and we promised each other that as a key to the start of a great friendship we would be 100 % honest with each other no matter what. It was kind of noisy in the bar and not the right time to tell Charles about my husband but I told him we should end the night and meet again for lunch on tomorrow. I told him I had something to tell him. I wanted to tell him about my husband so that we could really start off correct and he could make the decision whether or not he wanted to continue on or not.

I needed to be honest about my marriage and when Charles called the next day to meet with me, I was busy meeting with a college advisor and he was so eager to know what I had to tell him that he agreed to meet me on the campus site in the parking lot. He pulled up and I walked out to get in his car and I got straight to the point. "I know you asked me if I was married when I first met you and I said no, well I am. I've been married since 2001, my husband and I were high school sweethearts, separated in 2004 when he received a life without the possibility of parole prison sentence and I often times don't tell people I'm married out of fear of being judged plus I respect the covenant between husband and wife and this is why it's been so difficult for me to divorce him. I love my husband, he is my friend. He has done so much for me and my daughter we could never be enemies but I want to be completely honest with you as you have been with me so we're on a fair square."

Charles was quiet then he asked "Is he ever getting out?" I said according to the law of the land, no however I believe in miracles and I always pray for his release. I often times wonder how God feels about my decision to stay married yet uncommitted because I never want to deliberately disobey God but I never wanted to hurt Rico either while he was already being punished enough so I made a decision to move on in life as best I could. I knew I would suffer because of this but my main focus was to protect his heart.

I asked Charles how he felt about knowing this, He said "well, you should've told me but I don't think that it matters at this point because if he's never coming home what are you supposed to do?" He expressed how he respects vows between husband and wife and mainly because he aimed to do all the right things by Candy. I asked, who is Candy? that's my wife's nickname, he said.

He had totally committed to one woman for the first time in his life and told himself upon coming home from prison that Candy would be the last and only woman in his life but he felt as though his wife didn't have the same values or views concerning for better or for worse. "Looks like we're sort of in the same boat, Of course I still want to talk to you." I asked him if he still wanted to be with his wife. He told me no, that he was in and out of court with her & planned to be divorced real soon, he said she had done so many things to torture him and lie on him even before the judge that he couldn't stand her. I'd rather her just allow me the chance to be a father to my child, that's all I really want.

Charles said Candy did something very deceitful while he was in prison that changed the way he looked at her altogether. I asked what did she do and he went on to say "I believed I had a son with another woman and Candy would always tell me that she didn't believe this baby was mines so behind my back she had the baby tested for paternity and delivered the results to me while I was away in prison. I understood where she was coming from but she handled it all wrong. She should've never done that behind my back and it was only to prove to me that, she was in fact right and I wasn't the father but also to make me pay for believing that I was, during our marriage she claimed that I was putting this baby before her and she didn't like it" To further explain, Charles was sent to prison because of this exact situation. The mother of this child came to Charles home one night to pick up her son and saw that Candy was there. Candy and Charles had just started dating and she didn't want her newborn baby around any woman. This woman raised all kind of hell and called the police on Chuck that night telling the cops that he was keeping her from picking up her son and that there were guns in the house.

The police arrived and things didn't go well at all. Charles home was searched large amounts of money and guns were found. Chuck was taken away to jail that night for domestic dispute and later charged with possession of guns and drugs. This caused a lot of friction between all parties involved and the fact that Chuck was still willing to be a part of what he thought was his sons life after the mother did what she did and he was sent away to prison. That didn't sit well with Candy. She felt he should've abandoned them both and she went to no extent to reveal this woman to be a liar. For Charles it was about more than that, He prided himself on being a great father if given the opportunity and what Candy did behind his back, he felt it was dishonorable and it really hurt him but Charles said Candy was immature like that in a lot of ways.

He believed his wife was attracted to the lifestyle that he could provide before prison and once he came home it wasn't that simple to piece things back together again so quickly. He wanted to move different and slower but things just got really difficult between the two. She didn't have the patience to wait until something changed for the better. She got pregnant within months of him being home and things moved fast. Charles said he prayed for all of what happened to happen while he was away. It was a dream to have a baby girl. They both were very happy to have this miracle on the way but this came along with a lot of arguing and fights, mood swings, tempers, ups and downs. Chuck said that Candy was spoiled and vain and she would often use their daughter as bait to get a reaction out of him. She knew how much he loved & adored their child. I asked him, "How does Candy feel about you living with another woman?" He said "She left me, not knowing or caring if I had some place to go or food to eat so I could care less about how she feels about me living with another woman. There were days I slept in my car" Charles and I both were dealing with the pains of division within our families. He never signed up to be without his wife or daughter and I certainly never saw my husband and I being separated by a judge. No matter how you look at our circumstances one thing that I could be assured of and that was that God was still very much in control of both of our lives and his will for the both of us would trump our ideas every time.

Charles said "I haven't smiled much lately but meeting you has but a smile back on my face." I was fulfilled in knowing that I had given him a reason to smile again. He would always say how happy he was that we met and to be honest coming from a relationship where my trust was broken and my self-esteem was shattered he made me smile bigger than I had in a long time too.

---Facts over feelings, No matter how lonely you feel, after leaving a damaging relationship it is imperative that you take some time to love on yourself before entering another relationship, you will make better choices---

Life Lesson 6 – Never assume that the man you met, is the man that will stay.

The more Charles and I talked the closer we became and the more he couldn't go a day without wanting to see me and spend time with me. This man gave me the attention I had been longing for. He always made me feel so special as if there was no one else in his life. Charles was so sweet to me, he knew just what to say to make me blush and I loved the fact that he always made time for me. He talked to me every day, from late night hours to early mornings which made me curious being that he lived with a woman. I honestly expected days where I wouldn't be able to reach him but he always answered when I called. I guess they really were co-existing in the same household.

Charles told me that he had asked around about me to a few of his closest friends to make sure none of them actually knew me. One day he took me to one of his homeboys club and I mentioned to Charles that I knew of him through a mutual friend. I had been around him a few times, seemed like a cool guy. Chuck would take me to a few local bars but I didn't realize it was to show me off or maybe to see if I had been with any of his homeboys before. Didn't bother me either way, I wasn't the type of female to be with a lot of different men. We were now hanging out pretty often and our feelings for each other grew stronger by the day.

I learned his behavior & his moods so it was hard for him to hide how he truly felt especially regarding certain things. I would ask him if there was anything he wanted to talk about because more often than usual he appeared to be down and depressed. Within a year from getting out of prison he began to rapidly lose weight & even from the time I met him he had lost a ton of weight and he didn't like it. I could tell that his self-esteem was getting low and Charles was quite a confident man when I first met him, borderline arrogant to say the least. He knew what he could offer and he knew how to hustle hard to get everything he wanted in life so I never got the impression of low self-esteem from him until his physical appearance started to change, that and his pockets not being as filled as usual was a different type of struggle for him. Charles told me that from the age 14 he's been on his own, making his own way in life. He was always able to provide himself with the finer things in life. He was quite the hustler I must say.

Charles was always in agony due to his gunshot wounds, he had bullets & bullet fragments still lodged into his body particularly near his spinal area. The only option to help alleviate most of the pain was to have surgery to remove the bullets and fragments but that could end in him being paralyzed and neither him or the doctors wanted to take that risk so he dealt with the pain daily and this made him even more miserable and mean. I saw a rapid change happening, he became very agitated & angry! He would visit his doctor's office frequently and he was placed on some high dose pain medication to help him manage the pain and that's really when the weight loss occurred. Charles would consume those pain meds on top of not properly eating and just plain ole stressing, not a good combination. Although we were spending a lot more time together he was so highly medicated that he would often times fall right to sleep whenever we would get together, even at red lights while he would be driving, It was bad. Chuck just wanted to be with me.

Charles financial situation started to get better and he was now better focused but the stress of not being able to see his daughter remained. He would constantly argue with the mother of his child, every single time they talked. Just a phone call from her would immediately change his entire mood and I could see frustration take over his face. I knew that even though he told me otherwise that there had to have been some feelings for her still, because even though he was living with another woman, Candy controlled a lot of his emotions. She had his baby girl and when he would ask to see his daughter the answer always ended in No.

One day she finally agreed to let him see his baby but he had to drive to Ohio and stay the night in order to do so. At the time Chuck was driving a rental that I got for him so he asked me if he could drive it down to Ohio that he was finally getting the chance to see his baby girl and of course I didn't mind. I told him sure you can, absolutely. I was so happy that he was finally able to see her. I didn't know about him staying the night though to be honest there were a lot of things I still questioned about it all. I thought to suggest a hotel but I didn't want to further complicate things for him so if he needed to stay so be it I realized he didn't need to drive there and back in one day after taking meds anyhow.

I told Charles "hey, just enjoy your baby honey and you can call me if you need to." I made it a point not to contact Charles that entire day on to the night. Of course I missed him, we usually talk every day but I was giving him the time he needed to spend with his baby. I got a call from Charles that next day early and he's telling me how he got into a huge argument with Candy and left. What was supposed to be a couple of days of quality time turned into less than 24 hours. Charles said that the whole time he was there she wanted to question him about different females and argue with him, he tried to ignore her and focus on spending time with his baby. Chuck didn't even like raising his voice in front of his daughter that's how protective he was but Candy would not let up and when chuck dosed off to sleep there was her opportunity to snoop. She went out to the car rental to gather up all the information she could. Finding the rental agreement inside the car she came back inside waking him up, waiving this paper asking him who Tyria was? Is this your new Girlfriend? He begged her not to start any arguing and fighting in front of their child but she was getting even the more upset that he wouldn't answer her. She told him she wasn't giving him back the papers so that he could leave so he left anyway but not before grabbing her cell phone off the table and hitting the road. Maybe he wanted to get even since he now had to drive all the way back home without documentation of insurance or registration for this vehicle. Why did he do that? I don't know but he drove all the way back to Detroit with her cell phone in the car and his first stop was my place.

Very frustrated he tried to explain to me what happened and just how obnoxious Candy was being. Charles and I are sitting in the car in the driveway and I'm telling him you need to take that girl her cell phone back or drop it off at her parent's house but don't keep it. We weren't even conversing for more than 20 minutes before a car pulls up blocking the driveway to my parent's home and out hops Candy yelling at Charles to give her cell phone back. We both got out of the car shocked that she was there and she walked up on Charles and started punching him several times while cursing him out. I didn't say a word, I turned to Charles and said "give her phone so she can leave."

She went back to her car, rolled the window down and started yelling things at me like, "You betta be lucky, you gonna get yours?" "You must be another one of his bitches?" I've never met this woman at all, first time seeing her and I didn't appreciate nor take lightly the threats or name calling. I ran towards her and she quickly locked the door and started rolling the car window up. I was so angry that I hit the driver's window with my hand because I couldn't get to her fast enough.

She put the car in reverse to back up and pull forward as I'm walking back pass the car, then she hits the gas hitting me with the front end/bumper of the car hard enough that the impact knocked me down to my knees. She could've hit me way harder but thank God she quickly hit the brakes. At this point, I am livid! I'm yelling to my dad who's inside the house to get his pistol and come outside. She has now pulled off and circled the block a few times riding around taunting me with words like "Hahaha, You stay at home with your parents hahaha"... circles around again, "You're a hood rat, hahaha!" It was then that I knew what he had been dealing with this whole time, she had some serious issues and a different level of immaturity. I made her a promise that day that the next time I saw her that I was going to beat her ass and I meant it with every fiber of my being. I hit that window so hard my hand literally felt like it was broken but it was just bruised and had swollen quickly, in addition to the scraps and blood gushing from both knees from when I was hit to the ground. Apparently her cell phone was set up to track its location and she was able to find him immediately either that or the rental agreement which had all my information on it but either way I couldn't believe this girl showed up at my parents house and acted a plum fool. She drove up on the grass and literally assaulted me with her step father's vehicle, well nice to meet you too.

My mom and dad are both outside now in total shock! They threaten to call the police and report her but I told them not to, it's fine, I said. I'll be okay and I will see her again. Charles apologized to my family for bringing all this commotion to their home. He was completely embarrassed by her actions. He knew she was dead wrong for what she did. My parents understood that he had no control over the actions of another person so without hesitation they accepted his apology.

Now everyone's eyes are open and alarmed to pay more attention to this new guy/relationship that I was involved in. Charles left our house right after all of this and a few moments later he and I are arguing over the phone because I didn't like the way he handled the situation. Charles stood there like a deer in headlights while this girl did and said whatever she wanted to that day. I don't know what I was expecting him to do but I didn't appreciate him looking stuck. This was our very first argument and this changed a lot between us. I wasn't too sure if his heart was in the right place after analyzing this. Charles hardly ever wanted to show his face at my parent's house again. He would only come by briefly to pick me up or to drop me off.

    I began to question everything now, putting slight pressure on him to leave his current living situation and move out on his own. I mean if he really wanted to be with me then what was the problem. Charles was doing a lot better financially, he could afford it. To my surprise out of the blue one morning while his lady friend was at work. Charles arranged for everything to be moved out and hauled away to a storage unit. She must've pissed him off for the last time by attending that family trip that he didn't approve of because he ranted on and on about it. I certainly didn't argue the fact that he finally took the necessary steps to move on at the least it said to me that he was willing to leave her and move forward just us two like he said.

This decision cost him a lot more money than he expected so now there were issues of regret. Finding a place to reside in just didn't happen quick enough. Hotel expenses were through the roof and no matter how independent he was I still tried to help out as best I could. I would get him rentals and pay for them every two weeks so that he was able to navigate and move around freely. He hated the fact that I was helping him out in any way. This man had the weight of the world on his shoulders and as of lately every little thing would get to him. Our relationship became one where I was walking on egg shells around him just because I was often unsure of what mood he was in. I loved seeing him in a happy space, listening to music or something...music was his thing but just happy because he wasn't too happy to often it seemed. It was a matter of time before things did a complete shift for us as the drama continued to unfold.

Charles was getting calls from both women excessively and on top of that he started to question me about his friend out of the blue. The one that I barely knew from the bar. He was acting insecure accusing me of lying to him about not really knowing his friend that owned the club. He said that we both acted suspicious around each other not speaking to one another or never looking each other in the eyes. He asked me time and time again about this guy some times in laughter but there was some seriousness within his tone but still the answer remained "NO, I did not have sex with your friend. I do not know him like that." Then there was another guy that I actually had known for years. A friend of the family he would DJ our family functions, He and I never had sex but he accused me of being with him also, saying that one day at a bar he showed the guys my picture and the expression on his face told a different story as if he knew me in a more intimate way. I don't know why he was just now bringing all this to the forefront but there was no truth to any of it. Charles was searching.

He felt 100% right in his feelings about the DJ and I because according to him, he pays close attention to posture and a person's posture would never lie. He made up this story that DJ had admitted to having sex with me and when I confronted DJ about it, he laughed it off saying that it was absolutely untrue but however he didn't want me to have any contact with this man whatsoever. He wanted me to change my number to assure him that I wasn't talking to him or anyone else. This was his way of starting a new beginning since he had left his friend, he wanted to be assured that I was only dating him.

Interesting, because I was the one beginning to lose the trust I once had for him. He was constantly talking with the woman whom he had just left saying that he was just being nice, that she needed some time to get over him and he didn't want to just leave her with zero communication because that was his friend and they were together for a while. The now ex-wife and all her temper tantrums that she would throw, calling his phone back to back to back and sending random pictures of herself to his phone whenever she felt she was looking good or heading out I suppose, childish things to get under his skin and it worked.

Charles had a rapper friend and we followed each other on instagram. I posted a picture of my cousins and I on my page and this friend commented "nice picture ladies" and I replied saying "thank you, with a smiley face." That was it! One morning I grabbed us breakfast at his favorite breakfast spot before heading to his hotel room and as soon as I get there I'm confronted about this comment on social media. If ever Charles felt deeply about anything he was no hold bars. I couldn't even get in the room well before he asked me did I know such and such, I said "No, who is that?" Stop lying to me you know who that is you were just talking to him on your instagram page and before I knew it, he reached back & slapped the literal hell out of me. It happened so quickly and for no reason at all. I was more stunned than anything. I could not believe that he had just hit me so hard in my face about a comment on instagram. Charles said to me "I do not play when it comes to my woman and playing around with niggas that I know." I tried to explain to him that I didn't know this guy at all. I had no idea that was his friend but he didn't want to hear me instead he wanted to make sure that I heard him loud and clear.

---We are a sum total of what we have learned from all who have taught us, both great and small, reoccurring drama---

My face swelled up fast and my eye was turning really red until eventually it was a color blue. I wish I could say that this was a color I had never seen before but it wasn't. Unfortunately my light skinned got colorful when it would collide with fists. He went to get me ice as I sat in the hotel room processing what had just occurred and he came back apologizing for reacting the way that he did basically just saying he was sorry for hitting me but not sorry about what he said, he meant every word he said. I knew Charles was stressed beyond measures so I kind of just took it as a huge misunderstanding and I forgave him quickly. Couldn't go home for days until the night time so I didn't have to see anyone and this sort of cleared up. This was the first time that Charles had ever put his hands on me and what it did was awaken everything in me that I was use to. I didn't know him as nearly as many years as I did Ken so I was kind of scared at first because I feared what he was truly capable of. Charles changed from Mr. Sweet gentleman to what was his true colors all along, they were just waiting to emerge…and me… well, I changed from the woman that wanted a fresh fair shot at true love to someone's opponent again. We were never to be the same, every promise & every hope was now made to be a big ass lie. In my eyes he turned just like Ken within a blink of the eye!

---Psychological and emotional wellness is an ongoing process for everyone. It is strange…the reasons one feels she doesn't deserve better---C. Kennedy

Meanwhile Charles didn't have any place to go, I would tell him to go to his mom's house but he had an estranged, different relationship with his family it seemed. His mother was married to a man that Charles felt was jealous of him. He didn't like his step dad too much. He said he couldn't respect a man that doesn't work. He told me the last time he lived with them, his step dads son stole from him so he didn't want to go there ever again because that created a problem. Charles would stay some nights with me at my parents, some nights at his sisters where he kept majority of his clothes or at a hotel. Until finally after many prayers he got a call from his realtor about a house he was interested in & after a short application process he was approved to rent out this nice brick home in Redford, Michigan. His luck was just beginning to turn around and He was so relieved. He signed the papers and picked up his keys one afternoon and by night him, myself & his son went out to get cleaning supplies to go in and sanitize his new place. Charles was a very clean man, very clean and picky. After everything was moved inside and in its proper place I could sense him getting his momentum back, he was a happier Charles now. He constantly reassured me that things between us would be better now but above all he had a place to call home.
--We hope in all things--

Life Lesson 7 – Here we go again!

With Charles and I being so new in a relationship, I didn't want him to meet my daughter yet but we were together so much it was almost unavoidable. My daughter called me and said that she needed to be picked up from her friend's house and because Charles and I were together at the time, I had no choice but to ask him to stop by the house and get my daughter so that I could take her home. Nervously approaching my daughter's friend's home, my daughter gets in the car with us and is very quiet. Hi daughter, this is my friend Charles and Charles this is my daughter Shyra, they speak to each other. It was awkward but I understood my daughter which is why I avoided this. I knew she didn't care to meet anybody I was talking to at this time. My daughter observes me a lot and she already knew a lot about him before ever meeting him but when she met him she said to me "Mom, I don't like him," I asked her why and she said "I just don't because he looks evil." I didn't ask her to elaborate nor did I push them into a friendship. I simply listened to my daughter's feelings and I kept her away from him. I didn't feel he was evil but I do understand why she got that impression.

In confidence I tried to explain to Charles that my daughter wasn't really fond of him, in hopes that he would soften up his approach or act better around her but he took it all the wrong way and started to say things like "well I'm not kissing no little girls ass and She don't have to like me, I don't like her either then." I would've never expected him to jump defensive and begin to act like a teenager himself. I felt my daughter was simply not ready to move on to someone else after I just ended a unhealthy relationship. However, Charles was offended & I get it but he was being very childish about it.

Even still, I made one last attempt to get us all together for dinner one day. It was my treat to one of my favorite restaurants because I wanted us all to try and get to know each other better. It was Charles, his son, me and my daughter. It was nothing new for me to be around his son. I had been around him a lot since Charles moved so I thought it would be a good time to introduce our kids to each other as well and to just enjoy dinner together but that didn't work the way I suspected. Dinner was strange and it seemed sort of forced, the only thing that was good about the whole night was my rotisserie chicken and broccoli.

On the drive back while talking with my daughter, her opinion about Charles did not change. She still believed he was an evil acting person and she had no real legitimate reason to believe this. It was just her intuition I suppose. I came to the realization that my daughter feels how she feels and I will most definitely respect her feelings going forward, which now puts me in the position to either allow time to create a better feeling for her or make a decision to leave this relationship.

Charles absolutely loved spending time with me and that made me feel good, even if at times he would treat me like crap. Whenever I wasn't there he wanted me near so I was always with him. My daughter being a high school student probably needed me the most but it seemed like every weekend after work Charles would want me to pack a bag and spend the weekend with him. I would always go too, my daughter was at a stage where she wanted to hang out with friends mostly so I allowed her to hang out with her new friends and get acquainted with new schoolmates on weekends and I would be with him. My mom wouldn't let her hang out too much so I never had to worry about her safety she was at home with grandparents most of the time.

I observed a change in Shyra's behavior at school. My daughter was always a scholar but I noticed she was meeting different people at her new school that weren't of the greatest influence. My daughter got caught coming into the school building smelling like marijuana one morning. The schools security officer asked her if she had been smoking & a tail of weed from a blunt was found in her backpack after it was searched. I've never known Shyra to smoke weed or to do anything of this magnitude. I was caught totally by surprise with the call I received but it awakened me to pay more attention to her and maybe that's all she needed was for me to be more attentive. Quite naturally when you have issues with your child you tend to talk to the person you're in a relationship with about those issues to sort of vent. I informed Charles that I would need to spend more time at home and figure things out with my daughter after this incident and he seemed to be cool with it. Of course he offered his little opinions but he was supportive for the most part trying to give me sound advice. I made a decision to stay home more often than I was. I would still visit Charles periodically but not merely as much.

I went to visit him one day and his mail was laying on the countertop on the kitchen and as were standing there talking I detect a piece of mail with an Oak Park address on it. I knew that he lived in Oak Park previously with his lady friend so how did a coupon from Bed bath & beyond make it here, it didn't appear to be forwarded so I kindly grabbed the piece of mail and put it in my purse just in case one day I needed it. Something felt different, I felt as though he was still talking to his ex but it wasn't until I logged into his computer that confirmed this for me. I noticed that she had actually been over to his house and on his computer logged in with her email. Her email popped up when I turned the computer on. I waited for him to be honest and tell me about her being there but he never did. It made me wonder if he had still been involved with her this whole time but to further validate what I assumed, I came to Charles house on another day and his side window to his home was broken out. His ex had been there and confronted him and she threw a brick through his window. He was on the phone with window companies trying to get it fixed right away. Why would an ex have this type of problem with him? Throwing a brick into his window, He wasn't being completely honest with her or maybe he did something to upset her? He didn't have an answer for me. He didn't want to talk about it claiming he was stressed enough and she was just tripping, he didn't know why she did what she did but one thing I knew for sure is that everything that happens in the dark would eventually come to the light and it would only be a matter of time.

Charles and I would distance ourselves from each other whenever things were getting too out of hand, giving each other space because we seemed to have plenty to argue about as of lately. There was constant tension between us because he didn't like to be questioned. He hated the fact that I would ask him about the calls or late night texts, bricks in the windows. The bickering, the arguing, & the fights continued. He would get upset with me about the smallest things and he would get mad at me for catching him up in so many lies. Then there was his OCD, the way he militantly ran his household. He wanted everything squeaky clean and in its rightful place, nothing was to be out of place. If I were to cook it had to be done in a certain way, clean and sanitize in a certain way and definitely do exactly what he says and everything would be semi-great.

Because of everything that was going on in his life with other women, he started to look at me with accusations of cheating. Charles was never the one to search my phone but he got annoyed by me, saying that I was trying to act all perfect and that he was sure that there was something in my phone that I was hiding from him. He snatched my phone to search inside. He started yelling at me about being a hoe after seeing one text. He threw my phone back at me as if he proved his case and the phone landed on top of the head, hitting me hard. I never realized how heavy a cell phone could be but my head started leaking of blood, an immediate gash had formed in the top of my head through my hair and ran down my face. No, I don't believe he did it on purpose. He literally just threw the phone at me in anger but it hit me dead on. My head was hurting so bad. He got upset because he saw a text in my phone from a guy offering to take me to Miami and he claimed that no man would offer to take a woman out of town unless he was sleeping with her so I must've been sleeping with this dude but that wasn't true because this guy did make me that offer and I wasn't sleeping with him at all in fact this guy was interested in me but it was nothing more than friendship. After seeing that we were even in his eyes. He couldn't think of another way to justify his connections with these women except that maybe I was connected with someone too. I didn't fight him back that night, I just cleaned myself up and he helped me get the blood out of my hair and that was that. This was the very next incident after the slap in the face. I knew this was beginning to be way too much. After that night anytime Charles would attempt to fight me, I fought him back. There was almost always a scuffle. After fighting with each other it was like a cycle how he would feel really bad & apologize and then we made up. We both have even cried in each other's arms after realizing we were creating big issues that always escalated into something way more dangerous than we anticipated.

Our relationship consisted of us two meaning I was always away from my family and I never really met his family. He was a very private person. I may have seen his family in passing once or twice. I saw a few of his homeboys but we had been together as a couple a little over a year now and we never mingled with many.

In fact, the very first time I met some of his family was at one of their family gatherings that he didn't necessarily want me to attend. I could tell by the way he act leading up to the time it was for us to go. I believe it was his uncle's birthday and before we left his house to go to this celebration, Charles and I got into a huge fight. Let me just explain it like this, If Charles called me a Bitch, I would call him a bitch back and he didn't like that. He couldn't control me like he wanted to so we were constantly at odds about his attitude towards me. Charles son was there when we fought that night before the party and by the time we left the house to go to his families I had a slightly swollen red eye. We would often argue & fight in front of his son. He was around us more than any other person. I remember his son saying to me "why don't you just be quiet, when he yells at me, I be quiet but you be talking back" and even at his age, he was right. I didn't always have to argue back even though at times he made it impossible for me to ignore him. I was really looking forward to finally being able to meet his peoples but I no longer wanted to go after our fight but he insisted I still come, so I went. Chuck never wanted me to leave him after we fought and with all that had just occurred, I knew that he wouldn't want us to go our separate ways.

 I felt embarrassed looking in the faces of his family members and speaking to them with my head held slightly held down. I was trying to avoid them seeing my eye that at any moment was about to turn for the worse. I kept feeling like they were all starring at me. It could have been my imagination but I felt like his sister and her girlfriend were whispering about me and I could feel folks eye balling me. I felt so ashamed, this was a fresh bruise on my face, I had no mirror and I was ready to go so I demanded to Charles that we leave.

 Charles had a bad temper that he was fully aware of and his family knew it too. He had a tattoo of the Tasmanian devil on his arm since he was younger. He had been nicknamed after this character because of his behavior. He could turn violent with the flick of a switch but at the same time he could be the most caring and affectionate person. This was a scary observation to have for the man that I had grown to love but it was real and what was even the more scarier is that with all of the threats and fights, I wasn't scared of him by the least bit.

I was fresh out of a relationship with a man that was much bigger than him and I just never learned to down back down to anyone. Chuck wanted to control me so bad and he even told me that he never met a woman that talked back as much as me. I guess other women that he dealt with, would simply tremble and obey if he got to the point of uncontrolled anger but not me and for that reason alone I was fuel to his fire. We were like oil and water... we would have never mixed.

I wanted to dig deeper into Chuck as a person and I noticed that he harbored a lot of things from his past inside and it was hard for him to get over feelings of betrayal. In applying for disability because he was unable to work, Chuck ran across some shocking news. A man that he believed to be his father was not and his mother withheld this information from him for all these years. Charles was so upset and disappointed. He went on a rant speaking about his mom in a very demeaning way and how she even mistreated them growing up, she was a former addict and the state took all three of her children away from her. He spoke very highly of the man that she was with at the time calling him his dad and how he took the initiative to help his mother get back on track, clean herself up to get her children back. Charles said his sister and brother were able to go together but he was separated from them in the system and that opened the door to the damage and brokenness that he endured. Charles made up in his mind as a young boy that he would live a life that protected him as best he could. He told me a lot about his up-bringing. I knew that he had did the very best that he could for himself. He was a decent guy considering. He was just angry at times and he could be really dark and depressed even to the point of threatening to take his own life. Charles loved his mother and family despite their differences, he just felt like an outcast because of his lifestyle and to be honest Charles had a certain belief about women in general that stemmed from his relationship with his mom. His own blood sister reached out to him because she had been in a fight with the father of her child. His sister said something really foul to this man and they fought and it resulted in her front teeth being knocked out. Charles immediate reaction when he hung up from her was "see, you don't say no shit like that to a man, that's what you women have to learn, you can't just be bumping off at the gums because every man ain't playing that shit."

After it settled in his mind, his brotherly instinct set in and he started to feel like he should do something and not let this slide. He wanted to address this man for putting his hands on his sister, he made a phone call to his cousin in whom he asked for advice but ultimately he believed in disciplining a woman for the lack of a better term. Charles made it very clear that he wasn't going back to jail and that was his main concern but he was stern in the fact of a woman's place and I wasn't the first woman he put his hands on. He told me the stories about his exes but I fought back. I don't have an aggressive nature but an aggressive mouth if that makes sense. I was always ready whenever evil showed up. I loved God with my whole heart but I was a sheep gone astray and I didn't realize I was fighting unnecessary battles and that some demons were more skilled than me. I hadn't been fed spiritually in a while and I simply could not handle this type of test without God. I tried to get Chuck to come to church with me, pray together because maybe we needed Gods presence like a deer panteth after water but he never wanted to go. I wanted to help Charles in hopes that we could be of help to each other but the more we wanted to make it work, it seemed the worst things got. I figured Charles was a lot of talk and I knew he just wanted power over our situation. He was all over the place emotionally making me out to be a fool because he couldn't keep his word and be honest as he promised. It was just games at this point and I demanded more respect than that. I realized that my relationships had become a direct reflection of my habits and not my values. Somewhere between us trying to gain a trust worthy healthy love, we allowed our past issues to arise. Which lead me to react in the same manner as I did before. I knew how confrontations played out in the past so why would I allow this pattern to manifest instead of avoiding conflict all together. This had become way too normal, I was in too deep after that first slap to the face and not leaving.

--Separated from God, Trying to face my troubles alone--

I reached out to Charles one day and he didn't answer his phone, very odd because he always answered when I called. I waited for a couple of hours to go by and still I didn't hear back from him. I thought maybe he's just sleep from the meds but after about 4 hours or so I thought again or maybe he's over this ex chicks house. I already had the address from the mail so I got in my car, put the address in my navigation system and there it was, parked in the driveway, the vehicle that I rented for him. He must be inside.

I beeped my horn outside of this place to get his attention. I saw someone come to the blinds and then walk away. I called Charles phone once more and he didn't answer, seconds later he comes walking out of the house to get into the rental. I got out my car with a crowbar in hand ready to swing on whom ever if things went that way. I did not appreciate him being there with her. He was much faster than me because he quickly came out, got in the car & shut the driver's door in my face. I felt highly disrespected as I'm reaching for the car handle he puts the car in reverse and I'm yelling for him to not to back up but nearly running me down he backs out of the driveway and pulls off on me.

I didn't even think, I just swung the bar at a vehicle in this driveway which was obviously her car, and her car had nothing to do with it. I don't know what made me do that but that's how I felt. I got in my car to chase after him and she got in her car to chase after me. We were all on 696 high way speeding after one another until she eventually turned around. I kept following him as he was going towards his home when I got there he wanted to fight me of course without explaining why he was at her house in the first place and why he totally ignored my calls. He had his gun on him this night and took it out as to show me he wasn't playing no games. Charles got agitated by many things but to be confronted about anything or caught, that was a no fly zone for him. He had an excuse for everything he did and when he couldn't offer one he had a balled up fist for that.

Let me remind you that because of Chucks prior injuries he walked with a limp so he couldn't run very fast, if at all. He would only beat me up if he could catch me. He would have to have me backed in a corner or played it nice to catch me off guard because most of the time I would hit him back and run off and that really pissed him off. Things did not get better for us, they worsened but I stayed around the drama for whatever reason and he stayed around for the drama too. It wasn't always drama between us. He was quite the charmer in the beginning and I know our intentions with each other were good. Life just kept hitting him with unfortunate situations and he had no coping mechanism. I've heard of the phrase holiday blues and yes it got serious for Chuck around Christmas time. I'll never forget hearing him say what type of man am I, if I can't even provide for my children. He had just purchased a luxury car, he was living in a beautiful brick home, he was paying his bills, what more could you ask for. I saw this man grind his way from nearly nothing to achieving in a year's time what most couldn't achieve within 5 years of hard work so he was definitely hard on himself but he was a go getter and he wasn't for the excuses. As a man you provide and that was his motto and he was always the one that people turned to for help so he was upset that he had no one to lean on. I gave Charles $400 he would never take money from me, ever but I wanted to lighten his load a little. He knew I just wanted to help alleviate some stress during the holidays so he did accept the money after rejecting it a few times. Truth is it was never really about the money, his depression was deeper than dollars but it certainly didn't help that every time he talked to Candy she would be on him about doing this and that for their child and he would stress out trying to give his daughter everything she asked of him even if he couldn't see her.

Charles was a good father. He loved his kids wholeheartedly and it showed. He was willing to do anything to be in his daughter's life. I sat next to this man as he whimpered like a baby in his living room, crying his eyes out because Candy was keeping his daughter away from him. I had never witnessed a grown man, in all of my years cry so hard at the thought of being a part from his baby. It was as if someone had died but that's just how passionate he was about his baby girl. Candy made up all kinds of excuses and after a while she started to say that it was because of me. She didn't like the idea of me always being around and she claimed she didn't want her daughter around me. I didn't know her and she didn't know me. The only time she had heard my voice in a threatening way was the day that incident occurred and that had everything to do with them two, not me. She dragged me in it with the insults and assault and yes I remembered how she played me so I was waiting to get the chance to see her again without a doubt. I couldn't stand her but I would never do anything humanly possible to hurt a child. Charles knew that about me and he also knew that she would ride this excuse out until she couldn't anymore.

His heart was broken. He worked hard to piece his life back together again. His son was there with him every weekend the only thing he was missing was the hugs and kisses and the experiences from raising his daughter. I noticed Charles was getting more depressed and more distant from me. Charles was very predictable, he wore his feelings on his sleeve so I knew when he was being dishonest or deceptive even. I visited him one weekend, his friend had just been murdered and it really messed Charles up because he had just seen his friend in fact he was the last person to see him and talk to him before he was murdered. His friend went to meet a guy and Charles suspected this guy to be the one that robbed and murdered his friend. Charles was not feeling good about this and he didn't really want to say too much about it to anyone because he was the last person to talk to him but he talked to me about everything. He even pulled up a few pics of this guy on social media and was telling me I believe he's the one that killed my friend. I recognized the guy immediately because I had seen him before hanging out. I told Charles how familiar he looked and I pieced together the connection validating how I believed he could be right about him being the murderer. Remembering this guy on the picture from a while back he seemed like he was capable of doing something like this. He was a little wild acting and the people around him were calling him crazy and stuff. Some people you meet and they appear to have loose screws and he was one of those people. Charles began to question my story as if I was hiding something about knowing the guy or denying knowing him more than just being introduced to him, like I said.

He got so angry he pulled his gun out on me and started demanding that I tell him the whole truth. At first I thought boy you crazy, I told you all that there is to say and he got more and more infuriated claiming to shoot me if I didn't come clean about who this guy was to me. I was scared to shits because although he had pulled his gun out before, this time I didn't know what to expect. I was telling him everything there was to know concerning this guy. Charles had that gun pointed to my head and he cocked it back as if he was ready to shoot. He told me that he would kill me right now if I was lying to him. I couldn't say a word, I just cried... trying to gather my next thought to explain that I didn't know anything more about him. I was out with a friend that knew him and we ran into him and he acted a little bazaar and that's how everyone treated him, like a nut case so I remembered his face precisely. He let up and finally took the gun away from my head. I had NEVER felt like he would actually hurt me until this day.

We were in his bedroom in a small narrow space on side of the bed, there was no running away or escaping him that night if he wanted to kill me dead, I would be dead. After he allowed me the room to move around, I felt different all over my body. I climbed into his bed and cried myself to sleep, praying. I had no idea where this came from but he could be like that sometimes a monster waiting to prove to someone that he means business. After that night we both pretended like that never happened. We never mentioned that night again, not to each other. However I did over hear him talking about it to one of his cousins over the phone, in a joking manner saying that he would end up back in prison messing around with me. I knew now how important it was for me to allow him his space. We came to a mutual understanding that with all that he had going on in his life it was best that he took a break to re prioritize things, the both of us and so we did. A break for us just meant I wasn't going to be coming over like usual because we still talked on the phone everyday and I still would see him but there was definitely a change taking place.

Believe it or not, we were both still holding on to what we thought we wanted. I think we went a few days apart. I hadn't heard from Charles which was not so normal he called me every day. What I didn't know is that this was his chance to connect back with his ex- wife. I called Charles phone one night to reach him and he didn't answer. I called again in the morning and still no answer so I called his house phone to see if he was at home and who answers the house phone but Candy. "Hello," she says, I said "where is Charles at?" and she said "oh he's sleeping" and hung up the phone on me. I called back but the phone rang busy after that and Charles still never picked up his phones to call me back. I knew we were taking a break but I ain't know we was inviting others in. I took a ride over to his place to wake his ass right on up. I get to his front door rang the bell and knocked a few times. Charles opened the door, asking me what was going on? I asked him why was she there and answering your got damn phone, hanging up in my face. I came to give her that ass whooping that I promised her. He told me not to start all of this and just leave. He expressed he wanted to spend time with his daughter, that was it. This girl starts prancing in the doorway with a bra and some boy shorts on saying "yeah, she wish she could look this good, tell her to leave Charles." Charles asked me to leave saying he would call me later but I told him "nope, I can't do that I'm about to beat her ass" I tried to get through Charles to get to her but he wouldn't let me pass, Candy continues to stand behind him shouting out anything that came to mind. "I thought you said she was cute Charles, She ain't cute! What do you do clean toilets?" As I stand with my scrubs on. I had no idea what she was even talking about but she was clearly searching and rambling on and on. Pretending to leave I walked away and she got more amped up and came outside talking more crap. I charged after her and she ran back into the house so fast. I couldn't believe she was talking all this trash but was scared to come outside and fight me one on one. I'm always down for a fair fight win or lose I didn't like her and I was so ready to get my lick back. I brought a knife with me for protection because I knew what I had came to do and I didn't know how it would play out for me so I had it out ready in my hand. Charles was blocking me from getting to her, he stood in the middle trying to stop me from getting to her.

He is now starting to get a little aggressive with me as I'm trying to get to her and then he kicked me, while I'm swinging at her I must've struck him in the arm because he started to bleed on his arm a little bit. Oh then Miss Drama Queen starts to yell at him "Your bleeding, go get the gun!"

I'm still trying to get to her but then I noticed his arm and I told him I did not intend to cut him. She went and got her phone and called the police, telling the police that I just stabbed her baby daddy, within minutes the Redford police were there and I quickly tossed the knife in his bushes. Only Charles and I saw that I threw the knife in the bushes. The officers approached us and after seeing that he had been wounded on his arm they put handcuffs on me. This little scratch as I call it was nothing deep, it was barely a cut but it did slice him. She's steadily yelling for an ambulance and acting all horrified but he didn't need an ambulance at all and he told her that. I thought it was hilarious how she switched roles so intensely. I tried to explain to the officers that everything was fine. I told them I had a previous altercation with the girl and this was my boyfriend's house. His baby mother and I don't get along at all officer. Not listening, the officer is yelling at me for the knife and I'm telling him, I don't have a weapon. He then slams me in the back of the police car and shuts the door. He continues to talk with Charles and Candy. I couldn't hear much from inside the car, but I could see them questioning Charles about the knife and I see his gestures, he then points to the bush where I dropped the knife. The officer spots the knife and picked it up to put it in a small plastic bag and took me to jail. The officer was really mad at me because he felt he had given me the opportunity to be honest and I lied about the knife so he didn't want to hear anything else from me, I was going to jail. I tried to tell the officer when we got to the station that he had this all wrong. I knew I was guilty of having that knife that day but I had been wronged by the both of them before and never said a word and if anyone was being abused it was me. He hits on me every other week but the officer didn't want to hear it and I know why. He told me if it was true what I've been saying that I should've called the police on him. I looked like the bad person and I had no defense. I didn't know what was about to happen to me. I had no defense for going over there and attempting to fight that girl.

All I had was my word, After sitting in this holding cell for the entire day, on the next morning they opened up the cell and told me I was free to go. What do you mean I'm free to go, I asked? You're free to go pending further investigation, the sergeant said. I didn't exactly know what that meant but I knew I was a happy camper.

I sat and I thought about every little thing that has happened since I've been in relationship with this man. I reflected particularly back on a hospital visit where I had to be taken to ER because I suffered wounds after rolling out of his moving vehicle to keep from him attacking me one day. In the ER I was approached by a hospital staff member who was sent in my room. She handed me her business card saying that she knew that I was in an abusive relationship and to call her and she would help me get through this. I said to her "I'll be okay because I'm never talking to him again" reminiscing on all the signs and hints to just move on. I had a conversation with my mom and my daughter in my parent's kitchen one day, they both were concerned that I was being abused and I said to them "No, it's not like that, we fight. He hits me, I hit him. I think you guys are reading too much into it" I thought about those couple times when he pulled his gun on me threatening to take my life and now I was the one sitting in a jail sail with nothing but my thoughts. Perhaps God was trying to isolate me to get my attention for the last time and after all those thoughts what hurt the most was the fact that he was willing to point out a weapon to the police and have me taken away in custody as if I was nobody.

I felt stupid and afraid. I felt like I had lost the fight. I felt betrayed by him and the officer was right. I had been with Charles over a year and out of all the times he spazzed out and we fought, I had no record of any of it. I didn't have a single police report because I never even threatened to call the police on him. This was just something that never came across my mind even in my relationship with Ken, we didn't play the police games. It was frowned upon to get the police involved in your most personal business. Issues are to be handled from within us, & if it ever got that serious, it gets handled on the streets. My mentality was a little off but I was conditioned this way. I know now, this is ignorance. I was free to go because Charles refused to press charges on me. They had to let me go.

I was elated to now be free and walking out of that police station. I called my sister to pick me up. My sister and my mom were on the way. I started walking up Beech Daly hoping that I could meeting them would make it faster. I do not like jail and I never imagined I would be going back after the last time but you can never be too prepared for the bumps in the road.

Waiting and walking, I wasn't ready for this conversation, I just knew my mom had some choice words for me but she wasn't tripping she just said, "I hope you have opened up your eyes to see that this man doesn't love you and he don't have your back." I could do nothing but agree with mom, my sister chimes in saying "anytime a man would have you taken to jail, knowing what he's put you through is not a man at all. He's a coward." I made up in my mind that I would no longer be a part of this circus. I had my family support and they were telling me to leave him alone and so I did. I went home, showered and laid in my sorrow. Not a word from Charles and no intention on calling his phone. I wanted him out of my life for good. Out of all the games this girl played, it seemed as though Charles was making a new start with his ex-wife. I saw a picture he posted of her on his social media with very kind words of wanting to do better for his family. I knew it was for one reason only and that was okay with me. I can't compete with one's family. I would now move on from the drama and the games. Days had gone by and just when I was getting used to my solitude and my peace. I started getting anonymous calls from Candy. She called me saying all kinds of stuff. Saying that they were working on being together and she wanted to know if I talked to him lately, I told the bitch to get off my line and that pissed her off.

She started doing what she does best, talking shit...saying things like "you need to get to know God and he will bless you, like he's been blessing me, I'm a Nurse" I have this and I have that. She stated that my daughter was a hot mess and gets into trouble and smokes weed, saying Charles told her that he could never be with me because of my daughter. I argued back, told her to stop calling my phone I would hang up she would call right back. I asked her "Candy, Why and the fuck did you run when I came for you and you called the police on me, I have nothing to say to you" She kept saying she was trying to get certified as a nurse and didn't want to jeopardize her clean record and that's why she ran.

This girl kept calling my phone and harassing me day after day after day until one day I get a knock on my front door, a black man delivered me a personal protection order. This girl was really attempting to be one step above the game because I was over the both of them and I had no contact with him or her whatsoever. I wondered how a person could even get approved for a personal protection order against me considering the real facts. I still don't understand that, she had to have known someone who was able to grant this, this was a joke! My family suggested I go to the police and report how she's been harassing me and calling excessively. I went to our local police department with my cell phone where I kept all the calls and text messages she had sent and just because she was reporting me I wanted documentation against her too. They allowed me to make a report on her and I even inquired about getting a PPO on her until I realized this is really silly. There's no need for me to go tit for tat with this girl. I was no longer talking to Charles and I was happy about moving on. I found myself back in an abusive relationship with another man, same problems, same issues, same concerns, different face. This was the time to look in the mirror and examine me and what I was doing to create these problems around me but I was too busy seeing hurt, sadness and being the victim that I didn't get the clearest image needed while looking at myself.

--Others will try and judge you and make it seem as though Gods inactivity in your life means he's absent but you have to know that God never leaves you, He's just waiting to be invited back in to your life--

A month had gone by and I was doing just fine, me myself and I. I wasn't getting anymore phone calls and then boom, Charles called my phone. I hadn't talked to him in all this time and he called me anonymously. I answered and on the other end was his voice, a voice I didn't want to hear. I still had feelings for him of course and he left me feeling like everything I had done and everything we had been through was all a façade and cover up for how he was really feeling inside. "What do you want Charles?" he said, "I want to apologize for how I treated you and let you know that I miss you." "Oh, now you want to apologize huh, why after what you thought would work out, didn't. Now you want to come back to me when you realize she didn't really want you to begin with.

How am I supposed to feel about everything you've done?" Charles tried to explain, "It's not like that Tyria. I really am sorry and I love you and I miss you and I should have never played you like I did, I was just trying to be a family again." OK so go ahead try harder because I'm good! I hung up the phone in his face. He didn't call back but Charles started texting me throughout the day and again at night. Telling me how much he missed me and to give him another chance. First night, Second night, third night No reply and then I get a call again. "Please, Tyria I just want to see your face, please meet with me so that I can talk to you face to face" as much as I wanted to continue to be short in my responses and not say much of anything back to him a part of me felt relieved. I was happy that they didn't work and he was able to see her for who she was but it didn't help to know how he treated me in the process. I agreed to meet him to talk face to face. My heart wanted to hear what he had to say. I needed to hear from him that I meant more to him than what he pretended. Maybe my purpose was esteem driven but either way. I was happy to hear those words and I wanted to face him and my feelings head on. I knew we were over but I gave him a chance to meet with me.

I met Charles in a CVS parking lot, he was not coming to my place neither was I going to his. We talked in this parking lot for about an hour about all that had unraveled. Charles never would admit certain things but he couldn't deny them all. From the very first conversation with him, I've known him to be nothing but genuine about his feelings and he poured out his heart in the parking lot that day. I wasn't sure that I could ever trust him again but all he was asking of me was another chance to little by little & step by step work on our friendship again but let's face it things would never be the same. Candy didn't want Charles. She wanted to know that she could have him and that she could take him from me. I had never met a person so vindictive, childish and jealous acting...but Charles feelings was invested and he really was willing to take any and all risk to have his family back. Reality is, I couldn't possibly move on with Charles, this is a woman he has a baby with and therefore he has to be involved with her in some way, shape or form for the rest of his life. He assured me that she was completely out of his system and he had messed up with me trying to do what he thought was the right thing. We both had no idea on what to do next. Truth is I really did love him and I missed him so much. I wanted to give him another chance to make things right but the first sight of deceit I made it very clear to him that I was done trying with him for good.

---Is it the last straw that broke the camel's back? ---

I never guaranteed my whole heart would still be involved like it was before but I was willing to try. Charles wanted to prove to me that he meant every word he said to me in his apology to do better and he put forth an effort I must say. He wanted to show me the extra love, extra care and extra attention that he felt he lacked with me. Somehow I lost that affectionate person that he was in the beginning and I'm sure I contributed to that with not allowing him to feel what he needed to feel in peace instead of demanding him to react the way that I thought he should especially about his life and his family issues. Although we were just one step away from being done, I didn't want it to feel that way so I gave it all that I could. I didn't visit as often as I use to, it was difficult to explain to my loving and supportive family that I was back talking to the man that betrayed me but I was.

We were back dating again and working on mending things. Charles invited me to dinner with him and his son. We went to this restaurant, ate and had good conversations us three. This was our first date after our break up and we needed it. We even took a few pictures that day something we had never done and we laughed and hugged each other close. After dinner Charles and I went for a walk at the park, we swung on the swings and tried not to make everything so serious like before. I was surprised but no sign of Candy, his ex or any other woman being around and that made me more comfortable but still in the back of my mind was the possibility. Charles could tell that I just didn't feel the same anymore. I still cooked him meals and rubbed his wounds on his back until my thumbs and hands would hurt but I knew it was different too. He even asked me if I were seeing someone else when we broke up. I was honest with Charles about communicating with others during our time a part and that didn't sit well with him even with all of the things that he put me through. I know that was something he wasn't expecting but I left it at that.

I was still willing to work on us to see if we could get past everything that had be done. Neither one of us was intelligent enough to forgive, forget and move on with or without each other so here we were, figuring it out.

Remember the pastor's son who I was not interested in, well he got back in touch with me from social media one day. We had lost contact for years but he was now living in California and I saw that he had a son and appeared to be in a relationship but he said that he wasn't, anyway I would talk to him periodically over the phone as friends. He was coming in town soon for his sister's wedding and said he wanted to see me once he got here. I didn't know how I could make it happen with all that Charles and I had going on but I definitely wasn't opposed to it. This might be the change that I needed, someone different to show me something different. I was looking forward to his arrival but in the meantime Charles fought through his feelings of me talking to others and I fought through my emotions of dealing with him and all that he had to offer. He had to learn to trust me and I had to learn how to trust him again. This was easier said than done for the both of us. I think we both were trying to protect ourselves and play it safe at this point. Charles would often question me about other men, asking if I was still talking to anyone. Have I had sex with anyone else at the most awkward times. I would still question him about the texts and if he were being faithful. We were a mess but still holding on to each other because neither one of us was prepared to let go.

The time had come for my friends sister's wedding and he had just got in town, he reached out to me asking if he could see me and I couldn't because I promised Charles we would have a movie date. I told him "No, I planned to go the movies with this guy I'm dating but since you'll be in town for a while, how about we link up another day?" and he agreed. I don't know why but I just knew he would be a breath of fresh air. Charles had previously asked me to go see this movie with him that he wanted to see. He saw the trailer and thought that it would be a great movie and so he planned a movie date. We met up that Friday night September 12th 2014 the film was just released. We ordered our snacks, popcorn and goodies and we sat at a Theatre in Novi and watched "No Good Deed" I felt very uncomfortable as the film progressed wondering why did he bring me to see this crazy film. It was about this enraged man who was seeking revenge on a woman, very toxic and not a good choice for us so I was glad when the movie ended because although it was a good film, it was not a good film. We didn't even discuss the movie afterwards so I wonder if he felt the same way I did but oddly enough it was his choice. I didn't go home that night I stayed the night with him. I went back home early the next day to get ready for this wedding. I saw my friend at his sister's wedding, my daughter was a host at the wedding so he knew that we would be there but I didn't talk to him much at the wedding or reception at all. I didn't want to be all in his face and plus I felt like he had other things going on as well but after the wedding he rang my phone saying that he wanted to meet up with me. That never happened because when I made it home to give him a call his phone was going straight to voice mail. We didn't end up seeing each other until days later.

It was on that Monday evening that I met up with him. I was very impressed by his conversation being that he was younger than me but he was mature and interesting. I met him at his parent's house which I didn't really want to do because they were my pastors back when I was heavy into the church. I went on anyhow with him promising that I wouldn't be seen by his parents and he was right. I went straight to his basement area and we watched a movie and had a few drinks. His conversation was so refreshing to me. We talked about life about God, we had real positive energy between us two and then we kissed and that was it. I was there at his parent's house for about 4 hours and during that time my phone had rang back to back with calls from Charles. I looked at the phone and sat it back down not wanting to answer it. I thought to myself I'm going to get in trouble after this for not answering his calls. After I left from there I called Charles back and pretended that I had been sleep. I was in my car the whole time heading home from Tony's. It was about 2 hours later from the time when he originally called me. I said "Oh hey hun, I didn't see that you called me I was sleeping just rolled over and noticed the missed calls so I called back." Oh okay I was just calling you to say Goodnight, but I'll just talk to you tomorrow, he says. Never since I've known Charles did he ever not question me about not answering my phone. This struck me as odd, "umm so you just were saying goodnight" yeah, he says. "Well how was your day today Charles, I haven't talked to you much all day." "It was good, Tyria, just feeling really tired so I'm about to go to sleep."

It was as if he was rushing me off of the phone for some reason (suddenly I make a u-turn to hop on the freeway) if Charles were tired he would normally fall asleep with me on the phone so this was different and the fact that he didn't question me at all about not answering his calls & not to mention him being extremely tired that he needed to get some rest, right away. I guess I could have taken what he said at face value especially being that I had just left someone myself but my female intuition kept saying to me. He's on some bullshit, ride over there and see what this is all about. I swear I should've turned around at least twice as I could hear a small voice in the back of my head telling me, it's not worth it but I wanted to know if Charles would have the audacity to have a woman at his house after all that he had promised. I wanted to see with my two eyes for my sanity so I kept on driving and my adrenaline was rushing.

I ended the call with Charles as he wanted but it didn't matter because I was on my way. It was less than 20 minutes from hanging up the phone with him that I was at his home, wishing he was doing exactly what he said. I pull up in his driveway and hit my lights so that he wouldn't notice my truck pulling in. I quietly got out of my truck and went to the front door where I could see that the kitchen light was still on. I didn't knock or say a word. I put my ear to the window so that I could listen inside and I heard the TV going and then the kitchen light goes off. Maybe he's preparing for sleep, no worries..then as I lift my ear to walk away and leave, I hear a females voice giggling and I hear Charles talking as well, at first I thought he must be on the phone and on speaker because there were no other cars outside his home so I continued to listen on quietly. I went around to his bedroom window where I could hear more clearly, the bedroom window was cracked not even knowing what was being said all I know is that I heard a woman inside the house with Charles and then I start to hear these noises. It sounded like claps coming from his den area. I now have gone back to the front window to see if I could hear better from there and I couldn't hear much so I went around to the back of the house, closer to the den area and I listened on. I listened to Charles have sex with another woman in his den and I was stunned. I felt crushed as I heard the moaning and the claps from him either slapping her ass cheeks or hitting her from the back either way my stomach dropped to the cement and I start to react by banging on his window. "Charles, I yelled out open the fucking door" and he didn't answer so I went and knocked on his bedroom window a few times "open up Charles I know you're awake because I just heard you," still no answer. I had never felt like this before, this dude had big balls and he was just a liar, all that he promised and all that begging he did, I wanted answers and I knew how to get his undivided attention. I went around to the back to open his garage where he keeps his very treasured jaguar. He's for sure coming outside now. I just couldn't leave knowing this and not confronting him about it. They got real quiet in the inside everything was stopped abruptly. I went to open the door to his car and the alarm set off as I knew it would, in the passenger seat of his car was a small fake Gucci purse that obviously belonged to the female inside. Charles comes storming out his back door with a pistol in his hand. He came straight towards me in rage telling me to get away from his fucking car. I yell back to him "I knew you would come out now, I ain't did shit to your car" He had a look so furious on his face as I argued with him about who was inside and who's purse is in his passenger seat. Charles tried to tell me I was tripping that no one was inside and I needed to stop popping up over his house and just leave. I told him "I heard you inside fucking this person. How could you be inside the house fucking someone else and you were just fucking me the other night" He started getting more angry as I argued with him about his cheating ways. Then hear it comes, he said "what did you expect? I know you've been fucking around on me too." What are you talking about, you are not about to flip this on me but he's getting so angry as he expresses what he suspects I'm doing that he begins to fight me, He slapped me and hit me multiples times in my face and my head and that is when I smelled the aroma of sex on his hands. Charles hands smelled like vagina and with every hit I smelled it, I was more than disgusted, I could have vomited. I said to him "don't put your dirty ass hands on me, motherfucker I can smell the sex on your hand, stop hitting me." This was all I needed to know and to see. "Charles I am done with you!" Okay well just leave Tyria! "I will, if you let me get in my truck" but Charles was steadily trying to fight me and he was near the driver's side of my car so I couldn't get in my car or else he was going to continue to fight me. I started walking down his driveway away from my car, still arguing with him. I told him he could have all the women he wanted because I had seen all that I needed to see. I wasn't even trying to get inside his house to figure out who this chick was, I didn't care at this point, I had heard and smelled enough. I didn't even fight him back I didn't bust the windows out on his car or his house. I was simply hurt, astonished and him coming out just made matters worse. I looked him in his eyes and he looked different. I saw a level of anger arising that I had never seen before. I was literally arguing with him from my already broken heart. I guess I somewhat believed him wanting to change his ways and only be with me.

Charles was getting more and more fueled. I needed to get away from him as he's waving this pistol around in uncontrollable anger. He took the barrel of the gun and hit my trucks window and my front windshield just shattered. How can I drive like this? He is livid! And I know why, I kept violating his space and he was mad as hell that I just caught him red handed sleeping with another woman. He kept trying to come after me so I'm walking away from him trying to get his levels down, I'm talking calmly now, telling him I'm just gonna leave and before I knew it while my back was turned I felt my body swivel. I heard multiple shots being fired, I smelled a smell of burning skin and I could see the smoke near me. I remember trying to turn around and look at him but I couldn't my leg was no longer to the ground, The man that claimed to love and care for me snapped and he shot me multiple times in his driveway, leaving me for dead.

--A gun being present during a domestic dispute increases the chance of homicide by 400%--Fire arms are used to control terrorize and intimidate the victim, 35% of all women killed by men are killed by intimate partners with guns. 10% said their abusers fired a gun during an argument---NCADV

Life Lesson 9 - Wounded

I almost collapsed! I stood as firmly as I could on one leg, feeling myself fall to the ground. I tried to gently lay myself down in the drive way, my right leg was hanging on by threads of flesh. I felt the blood flowing out of my body similar to that of a fountain. I could see and feel my clothes being saturated with my blood, it felt warm and wet. I couldn't believe what had just happened, I looked down and I saw my arm seemingly deformed and hanging over my chest on a limb. The shock of it all could've killed me, I was so scared. I remember crying out "Oh Jesus" not even knowing what to say next but my spirit was in pain and groaned for me, as I thought to myself "Why did I come here?" then I heard God whisper in my ear "you're going to be okay" All of sudden I felt a peace come over me as if the world had just paused for a second. I was as calm as I could possibly be. I continued to lay in silence and it seemed as if moments had gone by before I heard movement again but that was just me going in and out of consciousness.

He handed this young lady her purse and said "here, baby girl you can just leave." I saw her shadow as she stood nearby & I heard her footsteps as she walked away. His next words were "See I told you!" followed by "Oh my God, what have I done!" then he came closer and said to me "come on baby just get up, please, let's go in the house" as he tugged at my arm that was dismantled. I replied "No, don't touch me, that hurts." I asked him to call the ambulance but he acted as if I didn't say a thing and he continued to pace over me and talk to himself. "My life is over now, I'm about to kill myself" he said. "No don't say that." I said to him and he quickly rebutted "Yes, I am, what am I supposed to do now?" Again, I asked "Please call the ambulance, don't let me die here, please" again no answer but still he paced around me and mumbled words to himself.

I laid there trying to come up with a story to tell the cops if they arrived, I didn't want him to get into any trouble. One of his worst fears was going back to prison & I could hear the despair in his voice, he went from angry to afraid. I heard the sirens from a far, it seemed as if they were getting closer. I've never been so happy to hear sirens in my life. It was a sound of relief. I could hear voices and footsteps in the grass then I heard an officer say "we have a female laid in the driveway she appears to be conscious oh wait I have a male here" and bang!

I never would've thought that Chuck would actually shoot me. He must've been over his limit. I really can't make sense of why he kept on shooting. I guess he didn't snap back quick enough. I was lying in the driveway bleeding to death with bullet holes all in my body, having a conversation with the man who had just shot me. I asked him to call for help and he ignored me but then again I asked him not to kill himself either, I didn't know he would take that same 40 caliber weapon and put it to his head and pull the trigger only to drop right before me. The horrific scene and images of that night still perpetuates in my head to date. It was as if he was in a world of his own. Someone must have called 911, maybe it was a neighbor but the ambulance arrived and this might have been the longest and best ride of my life. The next thing I remember is being on the stretcher in an emergency room as they're cutting my clothes off of me to see where I'm wounded at. I was soaking wet in blood and drowning in fear.

When we arrived I was asked if I knew my name and if there was a close relative I would like to contact. I answered, "yes I'm Tyria and please call my sister" and I gave them my sisters number. The hospital staff called my sister and had her on speaker for me to tell her what had occurred and I said to her "don't tell momma but Charles shot me and I'm at the hospital but I'll be okay!" I remember them telling her that I had to disconnect now because I was steadily going in and out of consciousness. I'm being lifted up from the stretcher to a bed, I felt pain coming directly from my leg as I was lifted. I was screaming crying for them to be careful because I felt that my leg would just fall off to the floor as I could see it literally hanging. The Nurse assured me to keep calm. She told me that she knew what she was doing but my leg was in such excruciating pain. The next thing I remember is waking up in the intensive care unit at the Hospital. I wasn't fully awake but I remember seeing a few faces at a time. I was physically suffering so much. Discomfort and pain are my assuring memories of that night and of pain one could only wish one thing, that it would stop!

For my entire stay at the hospital, the waiting rooms were packed with family and friends that just wanted me to make it through. I was flooded with love, cards, gifts and get well wishes. The nurses had become familiar with my family and they felt all the love and appreciation we had for them. The doctors and nurses were constantly communicating back and forth with my family. One nurse reported to my family that I had been shot a total of nine times and it was all over social media within the next hour. Everything happened so fast that night and there was so much blood they didn't have an accurate number at the time. Yes, I had nine holes in my body but I had been shot a total of six times. Some bullets came in and out while others didn't exit until surgery but no matter the number of times, the real miracle was in the fact that none of the bullets hit a main artery! It was as if the bullets were strategically guided by the hand of God to detour and not touch any main arteries, nerves or vital organs and not to mention the fact that, that night in the emergency room, I died. I coded blue and a team of providers rushed to begin immediate resuscitation efforts. I'm not sure how long I was gone and I don't have some drawn out experience that came with it, just a ray of lights is about all I remember. What I do know is that there was a divine appointment set up from God above that took me from an apparent death to being able to breathe new life again and for that alone I am forever grateful. He gave me back my beaten heart and allowed it to beat again. The doctor also reported to my mother during the time of surgery that he may not be able to save my leg which could cause for an amputation. I was told my mother didn't take the news too well and almost sunk in her seat at the thought of me being an amputee. My mother requested of my Ortho surgeon if he could please try again and he says "yes I will, I am doing the best I can." I was shot in my femur bone the strongest bone in the human body and there was a lot of damage done as my thighbone was broken in half but this surgeon went back in to the operating room and he must've went with God this time because he was able to successfully repair my injury by inserting a rod in the center of my bone accompanied by some screws. My leg was back pumping in no time. I was shot 5 times in my upper extremity which made my upper right side numb and useless for the moment, and once in the leg, nonetheless I survived where others could have died, I didn't.

--In my deepest wound, I saw your glory and it astounded me Psalms 51:8--

I understood that I needed to heal in order to get better for myself and for my family & in order to heal I had to focus on my healing, and my healing only. There was a counselor sent to my room to break the news to me of Charles being dead. My family stood alongside me surrounding the bed not knowing how I would react to the news. They wanted to comfort me as much as possible. What they didn't know is that I already knew he was gone. I explained to the therapist and my family that I talked to him after I was shot and I watched him shoot himself in the head. Everyone was shocked that I knew all these details and never mentioned it but I was trying to make things easier for everybody. I didn't know how to start that conversation nor bring upon any more hurt than what I had already caused and experienced so I processed his death by not fully processing it. I worried about his children a lot. I had so many nightmares in the hospital room that Charles or some people he knew would sneak in and kill me while I laid helpless in the hospital bed. I was on so much medication I was seeing different people and shapes & writings on the walls, it was crazy!

I felt alone and vulnerable yet I was surrounded by so much love. It was the perfect time for God to speak to me being that I was still and in a position to now pay attention. My mind was always busy and for once it was still enough to seek answers. Even on the drugs, I could hear his voice so clear. God would often talk to me about many things, his plans for me and much more, I felt so unworthy. Each day my mind strengthened and my body healed a little more. Encouraged in the lord by day and gospel melodies by night, my hospital room had become my sanctuary.

I still had bullet fragments inside of me and I couldn't move my right arm at all. My whole right side was numb as if it was paralyzed but I could feel the tingling leaving my body slowly but surely, by day 4 my vitals were great. I was able to stand up with my walker and was even able to take my first few steps with a nurse assisting me. Doctors were amazed at my progress they would come in and crake jokes, calling me 50 Cent and Pac, it felt good to laugh again.

--Jesus said to her, "Get up, take your bed and walk"—John 5:8 esv

I was able to urinate and pass bowels by day six so with just eight days of being hospitalized, this multiple gunshot wound victim was about to be discharged. Mom had re-designed and decorated a room right next to the half bathroom for my convenience. My Dad had a new toilet installed for me that sat higher because I was unable to fully squat or bend my knee. My family had all the instructions and supplies needed to ensure I would be properly taken care of. Everyone was as prepared as possible and I was on my way home. Leaving the staff of the 4th floor of this hospital and the ICU was all smiles and gratitude. They had taken such good care of me. I couldn't have asked for better care. Being wheeled through the halls and then on the elevator to the main floor was a new journey of its own and outside seemed so different. For some reason the sun shined a little brighter. The thought of adjusting to life after all that I've experienced was painful but I was equipped to handle the storm. God fought this one for me in a mighty way however I was not prepared for the work I would have to do to get well, be well and stay well. The real battle had just begun.

Rumors were in the air and people everywhere were talking, social media was intense. I thought about my friend Tony, I knew that everyone knew about my tragedy and I was wondering how he felt knowing that I had just left his parents house from what was a perfect movie night and in the same night shot multiple times by a man. I heard nothing from his family or him but I'm sure he heard by now that I was alive and doing well. People showed me so much love it was amazing but with all the love shown there were still sprinkles of hate. My family did their absolute best to guard me from any foul tongue which made healing easier for me but there were some things that I couldn't deny hearing because of the way it made me feel.

I'm riding home from the hospital after being released and Charles is being laid to rest the very same day. How crushing as I'm allowed to be a recipient of Gods miracle working power, his mercy and grace I couldn't help but to think that my release was his goodbye. I felt a level of guilt because had I not gone over there, I wouldn't be injured and he wouldn't be dead. On one side of town you have my family celebrating the fact that I'm alive and home with all the activities of my limbs and on the other side of town you have a family mourning and in pain with no answers. If I thought about it too long I would drown in depression so I decided to do my daughter and the rest of my family a favor and heal as best I could, fight as hard as I could and live with purpose going forward.

Each day at home consisted of the highest level of pain that one could imagine. I made a choice to only take my pain medication when I could no longer bear it anymore so I slowly weaned myself off of the narcotics and I let it be. Every muscle ache, every pressure, every feeling like that of pins and needles, every sharp pain down to every burning sensation, I felt it at its rawest state. For the longest of time, I could only lay in one position and that was on my back with my right leg elevated. I was very uncomfortable and miserable.

My mom and my sister would take turns cleaning my wounds. These are the most traumatic injuries one could suffer in my opinion but they both made sure my gauze were changed and cleaned for proper healing and to make sure no infection could set in. I don't know what I would've done without them two and My dad, I know I broke my dad's heart. He told me to leave Charles alone, he even told Charles to leave me alone and we didn't listen. He seemed to be feeling a little down and out during this time. I saw my dad cry and I felt so bad. I hope that he understands that what happened to me is at no fault of his own. Despite statistics I never saw him put his hands on my mother. He's been a real good father to me and I love him so much for being a positive consistent loving example in my life.

It would take all four of us together to make life as normal as possible for my daughter who was now a senior in high school and graduating soon. To my surprise she maintained her grade point average with honors and even though I laid on my sick bed she didn't skip a beat. With homecoming and prom being right around the corner, she showed up and with her head held high. My daughter has to be the strongest youngest person I know. The way that she channeled her energy in a way that was helpful to us all. She endured with such strength and resilience. I was just happy to be able to witness those special moments in her life. She gave me more and more reasons for me to press on with perseverance.

The time had come for me to challenge myself physically and train my body again to do that which was once normal. Walking seemed so far-fetched but I knew I had to do the very thing that I thought I could not do. I was asked by a very skilled trained professional therapist upon assessing me...What were my two goals that I want to have accomplished by the time therapy was over? I looked at her and I said "Well for one, I can't lift my right arm right now and I need to be able to lift both my hands in worship to God once this is over and for two, I want to be able to put on a pair of high heels again and walk around." We both laughed.

These were my goals and I stopped at nothing to make it my reality. I worked hard at physical therapy 3x a week. I started off slow with learning to take steps to strengthen my legs and my upper body and gradually I got stronger and I got better. My faith had been reactivated and I started to talk to God more and more about my thoughts and my decisions and learning to trust him with my future and things started to go fast for me. Before I knew it I went from a wheelchair, to a walker, to a cane. I had even graduated to pool therapy to give me the extra strength and motion that I needed. I was conquering much with the help of some amazing therapist and my families support. Don't get me wrong there were a few times when I broke down alone in my room or because I couldn't do a certain exercise at home or just because tomorrow looked like yesterday but I never wallowed too long. I had that inner voice inside of me guiding me and helping me. It was all progression and I was slowly growing as an individual even if my body was at a standstill. I've learned that when God is involved in anything, what could've taken months or even years to recover from is now subject to Jehovah Rapha.

    I was in therapy about two months or a little less and I was discharged to continue doing at home exercises for strengthening and guess what? I was walking on my own with a slight limp and I was able to lift my right arm at face level. No high heels just yet but they were coming and I felt good about everything. I would only consume myself with positivity, the gospel, reading spiritual books and daily commune with the holiest one. I felt like a disciple again, I mean I had really got off track. The first thing I wanted to do was go to church and sit there in his holy tabernacle and just exhale. I realized how important it was for me to be intentional about new habits and create a new normal for myself. Church was where I started and the place where I could purge. Rid myself of any negativity, resentment, guilt, shame or un-forgiveness. I forgave Charles the moment I recognized God forgave me and I don't blame him for treating me the only way he knew how to treat me and I certainly had to forgive myself which took longer but I eventually came to the realization that it was my choices that showed me who I truly was far more than my abilities and as long as I could keep from making the wrong decisions, I could create a beautiful life for myself.

-The name of the lord is a strong tower, the righteous runneth to it, and is safe, Proverbs 18:10

Life Lesson *10*- Sent from Heaven?

I was back in touch with the preacher's son who helped me in a lot of ways in life in general. His conversations were a different type of healing for me. He never asked me any questions about that night after leaving him. He never said anything about it all. He let me go at my own pace and he offered me insight and a spiritual friendship and that's something that I had never experienced before. Most importantly little by little he helped restore my faith in men. I could've been on the front page of a magazine that headlined "middle finger to all men" but instead I was on a better road to recovery and it didn't hurt that we were very much interested in each other as well. I thought Tony must be God sent to have come into my life at this time of healing and help me in so many ways but there was still something different about the way that he communicated that made me question his truth. When we talked on the phone it would be for hours at a time but then there were times that I was unable to reach him for hours. I wanted to learn him without judging him but I didn't know if I had the power to try. In the beginning it was a lot of figuring things out.

   I hadn't physically saw his face except through face time since that traumatic night and with him living in California, we couldn't see each other too often so it was a blessing to have a long distance friend that I could kind of depend on, it minimized the stress for me of the idea of being with a man again and it worked for us. I had men coming out of the wood works confessing their love for me while I laid sick and afflicted saying that they were ready to do right by me and I was the one that they always wanted and some believed I was their wife but it was only Tony's voice that my heart would adhere to. My thoughts were exactly this. He knows god intimately and there's no way he could hurt me like I've been hurt before.

   I started attending the same church as before, Tony's parents church and they knew we were talking to each other and about that night when I faced death. In fact, I remember getting a face time call from the first lady and one of his sisters after coming home from the hospital they let me know that they were all praying for me. Of course I had some questions and doubts about the past and what took them so long to reach out to me but my faith in God, lead me to trust in his people and let my guard down.

All growth involves a risk of some sort and I was willing to take a risk on being happy again. Tony made me happy and I made him happy. We quickly began to talk about a future together. The first time he flew back to Detroit was in December to be with his son for Christmas and when he touched down he didn't reach out to me. I wasn't expecting this so I gave him a little time because I just knew that I would be one of the first persons on his "to see list" being that when he's at home in California we talk almost every day and the last time he saw me I almost lost my life. He didn't reach out though and I didn't want to waste too much time wondering why so I called him the next day and I didn't get an answer however I did see that he was with his son, the mother of his son and some other family members at a mall shopping, a picture was posted on social media and then I said to myself, this is it…He still dates the mother of his child, the answer to all of my questions.

I texted him that night saying to him, I thought that you would want to see me but I know you've been busy so if you get some time, reach back out to me. He replied the next day apologizing that he was really busy with Christmas and had to come here to get gifts as opposed to shopping in California and paying extra money for luggage carry-ons. I understood what he meant by that but there was still something missing to this puzzle but the last thing I wanted to do was investigate another man or situation. I asked him if he was dating his son's mother still and he told me that he wasn't so I believed just what he said. He actually got back on a flight for home and I never got a chance to see him that visit but he was coming right back so I didn't put any pressure on him, if he wanted to see me, he would have. This was kind of how Tony handled things. He only communicated so much. He was very reserved and quiet in the beginning but it revealed to me that I was not his priority.

Tony and I never really got to know each other's personality in the past. After my husband's incarceration he reached out to me to develop a friendship but I had a lot going on dealing with bull crap on every end, yes this was the same Tony that texted me out of the blue late at night and caused a big argument with Ken and I. I decided to give him a chance because why not, no one else in my life was worth the risk and besides the next time I saw him after years had gone by he was looking real good.

He was no longer the little Tony that I once knew, He was taller with this chocolate complexion, nicely groomed beard, he was all grown up. I developed a deep attraction for him. In fact, I never would've imagined that we would actually be dating at some point. He was very expressive in the fact that he believed I was his wife. I knew for sure God had a plan for us, I just needed to be sure what his plan was because as I said there were some unanswered questions in my mind.

I would shy away often and let things be but he loved that about me at first. He would always tell me that he wants me to be his peace in the midst of everything else that he was going through. I tried to bring him just that "Peace" and love. We weren't that serious to be worried about the uncertainties anyway but every day I felt a constant longing for him. Could it have been like the other times where I just needed the companionship of a man? No, I felt this was different for me. I was determined to give love another chance and his kind of love felt good besides I didn't want the enemy to take away my ability to love again and to love as passionately as I once did. I realized my faults and failures weren't hidden in the passions that I had but in my lack of ability to control them. I knew better and therefore I wanted to do better, I wanted to prove to myself that I was worthy of the best type of love, the kind of love that I knew how to give. There was an intimacy that we shared without being physically intimate. With Tony living 1,000 of miles away we had no choice but to get to know each other in a more meaningful way.

While healing my heart and body, I was also balancing this post traumatic stress disorder. I've had so many bad dreams about being shot up and anything crazy you can think of, I felt fearful in my sleep. I found it difficult to stop thinking about what happened to me on that night. I hate the sound of balloons popping or fireworks or anything happening suddenly, it scares me the most. I had to begin to feed my spirit with the true and living word of God which was able to do what it always has done for me and that's heal me from the inside out. I had a long way to go but with God I had the courage to try. Before I knew it those feelings of hopelessness and helplessness were fading away. I wanted to be a part of the solution and not the problem. In conversation with the lord he gave me three words, My Beaten Heart and from there my organization was birthed.

Nine months after my survival, with the help of my family, we were able to put together my 1st of many Domestic Violence events. It was held right in the lower part of my church and my goal was to spread awareness to this toxic disease called love and to give God glory for the things that he had done in my life. I wanted to help other men and women become empowered and strengthened to know the difference between what was healthy love versus unhealthy love. I was extremely nervous about airing my dirty laundry to strangers because if you weren't close to me you didn't know what went on with me but I knew I needed to be honest.

Tony came down to attend my very first event and so many others supported and encouraged me on. There was not an empty seat in the church café and as I testified and released the truth of my story from my lips, I anticipated my healing in its entirety. Many in the room related to me and many were helped in some way just by attending the event. It was Tony's first time hearing some of the details of that night because he simply never asked but it opened the door for me to be more verbal about my abuse to the man that I had grown to love. He was mostly quiet about it never gave too much of an opinion just a listening ear and that was even more important to me. I often wondered, "How does he really feel about everything?" I'm more of an expressive person than he was so I was willing to tell him any and everything that he wanted to know to finally let it all out on the table but it took some time and over time he knew everything that I had endured. Every hurt, every pain and he expressed to me his past experiences too. We had become the best of friends. Tony understood that on some days I needed him to love me a little louder than others and I understood that he had been hurt in a way that my love needed to be genuinely authentic in order for him to receive it fully.

Two people, two different lifestyles, two set of issues and we both decided to heal together. Tony had a bit of a different focus than me at the time. He would never admit to me but he was still not quite over the relationship between him and the mother of his child. I knew this to be true when she sent me messages on Face book. Tony and I were together when I read a message from her saying that he was still contacting her with desires to be with her again sexually.

I looked to Tony and I showed him the messages she sent. I was hurt when she said what she said. She told me that she knew what I had just been through and Tony was not a good person for me etc,. you know the whole woman to woman façade. I read every message and I let him read it as well. One thing I did learn was that I never wanted to be in the middle of co parenting drama ever again and I believe there was some truth to what she said. I decided to leave Tony that night immediately, I was very upset and I got in my car when he came after me asking me not to go and not to listen to her and to give him a chance. He asked me to delete messenger on face book so that she had no way of contacting me again that it was just a deplore to try and hurt my feelings and distract him from being happy.

I didn't know if I should or shouldn't leave. I just knew that I did not want to be going through anything remotely similar to what Charles and I had been through with his baby mother and it gave me an instant headache and flash black. I asked Tony to give me some time as I sat in my car and cried because I was so confused. She had the proof that he had reached out to her and it was shocking because he showed me no sign of wanting to be with anyone other than me. I was totally blinded by this. He was so patient and loving towards me, I know this can't be a fraud. I didn't want to think about anything else that night, I pulled off in my car and I went home and cried some more. Tony was determined not to let me leave him or us in this way, constantly reassuring me that this text was nothing other than the result of him having too much to drink one night. He apologized and begged of me to believe him. I already was feeling like things just weren't adding up with him. From the things he would do and say on social media. His actions wouldn't match up with his words at times but his words were so satisfying and whenever we were together it was a lovely experience for me.

I had a lot to think about. I had quietly loss my confidence in us but when you're taught faith and forgiveness it's hard to allow something so meaningless to completely separate the possibility of what could be. I was back talking to Tony the very next day and he promised me he would never do anything to intentionally break my heart. I believed him and I washed away all that she said. He was good to me at the end of the day and better than I had ever experienced so what did I really have to lose?

Life for me was pretty much back to normal, well as normal as it could be. I had just been cleared from my doctors, at my last appointment. My orthopedics doctor just wanted me to check back every 6months to get an image of my leg with the rod in it to make sure there was still a pulse and everything looked good. I was back to work fulltime as a medical receptionist and I was happy with my new friend. Tony wanted me to visit him for the first time in California so that would mean I would have to get on the plane by myself and go to an unknown land with a man. I told my parents about him and about the visit and they didn't mind me visiting him at all. They knew as well as my daughter the feelings that I developed for him and I guess they too found some sort of comfort in knowing that at least he had a relationship with God.

I booked my flight and was headed to the sunshine state. I was no longer walking with such a limp anymore and I could even put on a small heel so I was ready to enjoy myself. It was a quick weekend trip, he picked me up from the airport and we went to his friend's home. It was closer to the airport near LA so we hung out there until it was time for me to leave. I had a really good time. We went out to a lounge to have a few drinks, listened to music and chilled out. We were really well with each other. We took pictures and we went to a mansion party one night, the next day we walked up the boulevard and talked more with each other, stopped in a few places site-seeing and I enjoyed the best yummiest cheese fries I've ever had at this restaurant along the way. Tony got a little sick to his stomach during my visit so we didn't do too much my last day there. We relaxed mostly but it was enough for me being with him for the weekend and of course all good things come to an end and it was time for me to go. He drove me to the airport & with a sensual kiss and the most teddy bear hug, we said our goodbyes.

I was back to Detroit by Monday to get ready for work. Things between Tony and I were going great. He would come to Detroit more often than I would visit him. He was really close with his family here and whenever he wasn't handling business, he would come to visit everyone. He was very business minded, he had his head on straight and he was successful in all of his ventures. He was a man of good character as far as I could see but one thing... I never understood why I had to ask him if he had another child.

I knew about his oldest son but I saw a younger baby boy with his sister and I heard mention of another grandchild from the pulpit one day. I found it odd and I didn't know how to bring it up to Tony because I was under the impression that we didn't keep things from one another but again he communicated how he wanted to and the only way I would get my answer is if I were to directly ask him and so I came out with it one day. "Tony, Do you have another son?" we were over the phone and he said "yes, I have another son." Call me crazy but why did I have to ask you this and Tony said "He thought I knew" There were no pictures of this baby on his social media pages and as much as I talked to him he didn't even talk about him so how would I have known. I started to learn his behavior and how he operated with personal matters and how he wanted to portray a certain image. I firmly believed that's how he was raised as a pastors kid but for some reason I believed he wasn't acknowledging his youngest son to spare the feelings of his oldest sons mother, being that he got another woman pregnant while they were in the off stages of their relationship. I'm not sure the exact reasons but this was one more thing that made me look at him differently but I could never deny his honesty, he was always very truthful with me whenever I asked him anything. I never felt like he was lying to me about anything or anyone. One thing I know for sure is that he loved both of his children with his whole heart. Some people are just different, I was more of an open book not that I had too much of a choice but my issues, my insecurities, my concerns I was open to share. With us being far apart we could only talk to each other to gather as much information and trust for one another. We would be on the phone sometimes 7-8 hours out of a day, talking about any & everything. We would face time often, send each other pictures, whatever we could do to keep connected and close.

You never really truly know someone until you're able to be with them, in their presence. We made it our business to make more time for each other whenever our schedules would permit. It was summer when Tony came down to visit and this was the first time that I had come to the conclusion that I had something to deal with being in love with this man. I've always known him to casually drink, he kept liquor at his home, at his parents but it seemed to be just for fun.

I got with Tony one day and he must've been drinking before I picked him up because we met up with his brothers and they all starting drinking more and by the time we had left them, Tony could barely walk to the car and once he got into the car he passed out. I was trying to get him to wake up because I didn't want to drop him off at his parents (my bishop and first lady) house this way. Tony had urinated on himself in the front passenger seat of my car. When he finally woke up and got out of the car, there was piss everywhere... his pants were wet and my seat was soaked. I knew that this was a different type of drunk and I thought to myself...he can't hold his liquor, he never needs to drink again and I just laughed it off to be honest. I was more so interested in a clever way to get him in that basement without his mom and dad noticing but then the drinking became routinely.

Before I knew it, I had become the one that needed to help him so he didn't get drunk as much. I found out that his mom and dad did in fact know about his drinking habits because one day while sitting in their garage. His mom came to me and said "I'm glad you and Tony met. He seems to like you a lot and just maybe you can help him with his alcohol use. He gets stressed out about a lot of things and maybe you can talk to him." I didn't know what to say I just said "yes ma'am" because I knew he drank way more often than he should. Tony told me that he didn't have an alcohol addiction that he only drank when he came in town for sociability purposes and he considered being home in Detroit a vacation after all he was away from work in Cali. I believed him, he was running a school mentoring business in California and it was doing well so it must've been just casual drinking that would go too far at times. I mean how could a person function, run this business and do well in life in California if they were an alcoholic?

He was not that to me, he was a strong man of God that looked good and made me feel better and that's the only thing I wanted to believe about him even when he would get drunk and be mean to me and push me away. I told myself that he didn't actually mean to be mean, he just murmured mean things while under the influence.

He was still my King, he just needed some extra attention because he had been alone in California for so long away from all the love that he had ever known. He always wanted to please his family and a lot of the sacrifices that he made was for that reason, pleasing his family. It was taking him down to continue to hold up this torch and proclaim to be the great namesake when he was yet struggling inside. I wanted to bring out of him the very best that I knew he could be, for us and for me. In the beginning, I let plenty slide for the sake of arguing and just being afraid to address it but once the most darkest side of Tony was revealed to me and I stayed he got more comfortable with me. It seemed that once he knew that I was still going to be there, he always wanted to keep me close to him.

He asked me to move in with him in California. I laughed it off not knowing he was dead serious but ever since I met this man his intentions with me never waivered. He believed I was his wife and I started to believe this was my husband. I had finally got the divorce from Rico a while back and I was totally free from any titles or dark clouds that could have been hovering over me due to my choices. I felt really good about us...Tony wanted us to be together indefinitely and I felt the same way.

It didn't take me long to come up with a yes. I just needed to know how we could make it happen with all that I've been through. How do I ask my parents for their blessing and my daughter would need to come with me as well. My mom had become very protective even though I was grown. She lost her son and almost lost her daughter due to violence. Tony was no stranger to any of us at this point & it was easier than I expected to get everyone's blessings. He told his parents and they were okay with it too. Tony and I discussed in grave details how things would go and we both were ready to start a future together. I was now making the necessary preparations to make a life altering decision and that was to move thousands of miles away from the only home that I've ever known with my man. I had given my job a month notice. I saved up some coins and I knew that once I got to California I could always find work there in the medical field. I handled everything business wise that I needed to.

The only thing I worried about was my organization, it had been birthed here in Michigan and was doing really well advocating and bringing awareness to Domestic Violence and helping victims from all over which made me think on a broader spectrum, this need is not Michigan specific. I began to contact different organizations for Domestic Violence in California and made some connections with a few coalitions there so I was confident that I would still be fulfilling my purpose no matter the location.

Here's the hang up! One night prior to me leaving there was a prophetic service being held at my church and as I walked by the prophet to put my offering in the basket. He stopped me dead in my tracks and the prophet said to me. "God said don't do it!" My heart dropped knowing exactly what he meant but he continued on and said. "He's not ready" and it was as if the church took a deep breath at once and it got quiet and he started to elaborate, "what, is he here? I know what I heard God say" and I just continued to walk to my seat. I've never felt so called out before in my life no one in that church knew that I had plans to move to California besides Tony's parents. The church knew that Tony and I were dating and maybe that's where the sigh came from.

I immediately called my bishop and first lady before they could even make it home from service because I wanted to know their opinion about what was just said at service. I was in tears as my bishop told me that sometimes prophecy could be off and he doesn't know why that was said to me but all he knows is that Tony really loves me and if he were to give me any advice it would be to not worry about what was said and to continue to be there for each other and love one another and to move as planned.

My bishop had given me his blessing and even though it didn't 100% clear things up for me I was confident in his confidence in us and I did as my bishop advised. I talked to Tony about it that night also and he also told me not to worry that he was in fact ready for me and for love and not to let every word that I hear from a prophet be the final say for us. I was super nervous but the plan was to move to California, find work & have my daughter enrolled in college there and then send for her later so I proceeded with the plan.

   I had worked my last 8 hour shift, everything was packed away and I was ready to go. I kept asking Tony, "Are you sure you want me to come?" and he was certain. The next couple of days, I was headed to Moreno Valley, California to be with the man that I considered to be the love of my life.

–If ever in doubt, talk to Jesus, Gods instructions are clear--

Life Lesson 11 - Ain't no love in California

As a Christian, we are taught that to move in with a man before marriage is frowned upon, it's shacking and God doesn't honor this type of behavior. Tony and I knew we wanted to be together forever and that marriage was the ultimate goal so even though we were a bit out of order in our approach and wanted nothing more than to honor God we still did what we felt we should do in our hearts.

It was a 5 hour flight...I had most of my things with me, the others were being shipped on a later date but there he was, I was greeted by my teddy bear. He picked me up from the airport and we headed back to what was now home for me. Every day was like sunshine from the skies. This man was so fun and kind to me that it seemed unreal. I had my issues with him do not get me wrong, there were different females that he was in contact with and his interactions with various women on social media brought on a lot of trust issues for me, it just seemed to be misleading and distasteful for a man that was seemingly committed to someone but I wasn't going to break up with him because of it. I just talked to him about it and hopefully my feelings would sway him to change. I always felt insecure in the fact that he had what I call a wandering eye. Tony had a sexual thing for women, he was attracted to everything about a woman just give him eye candy from a woman to gaze at and he was all in. I didn't know if that could be tamed. He gave me all the love and attention I needed face to face. I never felt like I wasn't enough for him but my concern was the level of respect he displayed behind my back. I was always one to figure out what I wanted to know by way of snooping or a good ole' persuasive conversation but it was hard to get through to him regarding his actions at times. It was something we eventually had to get over. Tony asked me to move in with him so to him that was proof enough that he only wanted me. He did at some point calm down with all the women. He changed some ways to make me feel more comfortable and so did I.

As we began to spend more time together, living together. I noticed his drinking wasn't casual, it was a bad habit. Tony never talked to me about his concern with me of other men so I never knew he had any thoughts about it, until one day he had a bit to drink, we were both drinking actually. I would often join him in a drinking because he was always doing it and it made for a better time to be honest but he wanted me to make out a list of the men that I had previously been with sexually. I didn't know that it was only to see if there was this one particular name listed. Why wouldn't he just ask me about this guy. I thought okay…maybe this is how he wants to know more about my past, open up and communicate more so I agreed to do the list and I asked him to do the same. This was a different Tony to me. He kept a lot inside pretending to be secure and confident in us, in himself but he was the exact opposite. The name that he didn't want to be on my list, was on my list. He suddenly got so upset with me, calling me a liar and a whore because in a previous conversation when we were just on the level of friends, I told him this person was like family to me. I've known this person for years and he has been a real close friend of the family. It was one time over 10 years ago that I had been with this guy & that was it. We've been nothing but friends ever since 100% truth. Tony didn't like it and he didn't believe me so he wanted me to leave his house. He called his parents to discuss with his dad his reasons behind feeling so hurt. He felt that I lied to him, it was betrayal and there was no changing his mind. We argued and argued because I couldn't believe he was reacting this way. His list was way longer than mines the audacity to get mad about one person and I was playing it cool.

    It was as if he plotted and waited to get this out and he kept insisting that we could no longer work out because of this. I packed my things and he drove me to the airport. With tears in my eyes I got out of his car grabbed my suitcase and purchased a ticket to come back home. The idea of me being involved with someone that he knew of, was hurtful to Tony and he didn't even know the guy personally and this was ten years ago but that didn't matter either. It was just how he felt and I couldn't argue that. I never imagined that would blow up in my face in that way. He really set me up to find out what he wanted to know and that was okay because I never lied to him and I never intentionally kept anything from him.

I wanted him to know everything about me because he was so good at helping me get through my issues, I never wanted to hide a flaw. No one knew that I had moved to California but those closest to me however they certainly knew when I returned home. It was kind of embarrassing after being there for just 3 months to state that Tony wanted space from me. I called my mom and I had to explain to her that I was coming home. Imagine how this made me feel.

Tony and I weren't talking like we usually do and things were falling apart but I still believed in him and in us and I wanted us to rekindle things. Attending church was the thing that kept me sane and grounded and somewhat connected to him. We finally started to talk again, Tony could be very stubborn. He wanted things done his way. We both were on edge after this, trying to come to a clear understanding about where we stood. I couldn't seem to get him on the same page with me it was as if he wanted me to feel guilty. I didn't think that I did anything wrong but I did understand his feelings towards the situation so it left me at his mercy trying to explain to him how my present heart and my past simply do not intertwine. I worked so hard to forget about my past and the things that easily beset me that I just wanted a fresh clean start.

We had this thing that we would do by the pond. He took me there after our first disagreement so that we could talk by the water. That day I asked him to look at the pond as representation of a sea and I named that pond "the sea of forgetfulness" and if ever we were to bring an issue to the sea of forgetfulness, we would have to leave it there, never to remember it again. This was our pack and although we didn't go there too often, when we did..our issues seemed to creep back with us. Tony and I are both are very intelligent human beings and we have the spirit of the living God on the inside of us so it was most frustrating amongst all things that we couldn't conquer little battles that we were faced with even in our minds. We both were willing to try, knowing that we loved each other that much. We worked on building us again, from afar...Starting all over and forgetting about the past.

I would still visit him in California and we would still talk every day. We had already purchased a one way ticket for my daughter to come and be with us but I wasn't even there now so we had a lot to discuss. I mentioned cancelling her flight so I asked if he wanted us to still come there or what. Tony said he wanted me to come back, me and my daughter both just like we originally planned. He had forgiven me for what hurt I caused him. I asked my daughter how she felt about it and she still wanted to go but she wanted us to go with a plan of our own. My daughter had plans in Cali, fresh out of high school on her way to college where she could further pursue dance in Hollywood. My daughter had an idea and I found housing through airbnb, upon arriving our plans were for the both of us to find employment, save up enough money to get our own place to alleviate the stress of what could go wrong. My daughter had been to L.A. several times before so she was a little connected and ready to jumpstart in the dance field we didn't want any of this to be a hindrance. Come on we're talking about California, what is there not to like about the inspiring state of dreams.

With those plans set in motion I explained to Tony that we were willing to come back but we wanted to take things slow. He and I could date and be besties again and at least if I needed any help, he would be near. Tony promised to not drink as much and agreed with our plan, "Let's do it!" Tony said.

--You're not ready to commit until you come to terms with the fact that some things you love will change overtime and some things you hate won't—

My daughter and I were preparing to leave we said our goodbyes and again we get the blessings from our pastors and my family. Tony picks the both of us up from the airport to drop us off at the place that we had rented to live in. We got there and the conditions in which I signed up for were not as the contract stated. I didn't know how those airbnb's worked exactly but it never implied that there would be someone else there with us and of male gender. We did have a lock on our door but there was only one bathroom that we had access to and again, a man lived there. I was kind of scared to stay there that night to be honest.

It was a horrible position to be in because I wanted to play it off and act tough so that Tony didn't notice anything wrong. He brought our luggage inside and we got set up for the stay but deep down inside I wanted him to intervene so bad and he eventually did. He said "you know you guys don't have to stay here you can come to my place." My daughter said to me "mom we will be fine" but I was not okay with staying there knowing a man lived there and it was just us two. I pulled Shyra to the side asking her if she didn't mind maybe we could just go with Tony for the night and figure out another plan by morning. She hesitantly agreed, no one was quite happy about the fact that Tony asked me to leave his apartment in the first place and if anyone knew exactly what went on it was my daughter because she was the only person I would talk to about him and his behaviors. My daughter and I have always had the best relationship some would say that we're too close but I could vent to her about him and she would give me an honest perspective sometimes it would be in his favor and sometimes in mines. She was fair and understanding but she didn't want to be put in that position again, to be hurt. My daughter was also concerned about his drinking but she said "yes mom that's fine with me."

We left with Tony that night explaining to him that we would be figuring things out by the morning and when we pulled up to his place, he parked the truck and said he wanted to talk to the both of us before going inside. Tony sincerely from his heart explained to me and my daughter how bad he felt for asking me to leave & how he had done the wrong thing by me. His eyes began to fill with tears as he said he wanted to be with me still and have us both there with him like a family, like we planned and he promised to do right by the both of us. He asked us to stay there with him as long as we wanted, you guys don't have to leave. I want y'all here, Tony said. My daughter was touched by his words and all the emotion behind it but she said to him, I just don't want you to get upset again and we don't have anyone here to turn to and he reassured Shyra that he wouldn't do that to us at all. I had very little to say that night because I wanted to hear him clearly . My daughter spoke her heart and I thought we had finally come to a common ground. Things slowly went back to normal or should I say we were slowly progressing.

   Shyra and I both obtained jobs there, we were working at the BMW dealership in Riverside, meeting new people and establishing new friendships, it was great! Tony would have to take me to work and Shyra would uber some days because of our schedules but we were working it out. The only thing we needed now was a great church home. I couldn't believe Tony had been there all those years and didn't join any of the great ministries California had to offer so that was next on the agenda and we did, after visiting many churches, we believed we had found the perfect ministry to get involved with. There was this mega ministry in Rancho Cucamonga, Tony and I loved it there and Shyra too. It was on our heart to join and quickly get involved they were doing big things but Shyra and I next move was to get a car and then our own place. Our plan was still in motion but Shyra's school application was denied because you need to be a resident of the state for a full year in order to qualify for any loans otherwise you pay a substantial amount of money per semester so that was a negative for us, we couldn't afford that. Other than that things were looking up for us but the business was slowly looking down for Tony.

   The after school program in which he ran was at risk of being permanently closed down by the government for lack of funding approvals. It was beginning to be a stressful time for him and he still had his weekend alcohol habits. I helped out as much as I could with what he allowed me to assist with. Tony was also sort of controlling and the type of person that was "always right" so we were constantly in a combative state and I felt like everything I said was challenged. It was almost as if we were in a competition at times and I didn't understand why. I had a voice but I've always had a voice so he rejected a lot of my help when really all I wanted to do was help. We argued often and it's okay to disagree but we didn't know how to respectfully disagree. If he had been drinking it would be bad. He was stuck on being the male authority and of course a woman has her place and that all worked while I was loving this new man of God that I had been blessed with but after a while, drunk or not this was not about to be my new normal. I started to get back with the son of a preacher & in all honesty, I hated to go back and forth with him, lord knows I avoided what I could with all my might but I felt provoked often and I wasn't with the shenanigans anymore.

There was a side to me that Tony wasn't ready for and it wasn't so nurturing like before. I watched him drink all day and night. He wouldn't even wake up to handle business until 4 or 5pm. If there were meetings he sobered up and if there was a tutoring session he would be on board but he was literally a functioning alcoholic. His intake was detrimental. We had our good days and we had our bad. He became more and more verbally aggressive towards me in a demeaning and disrespectful way and I would tell him, "Tony that hurts my feelings to have you treat me this way whenever you're drinking" which was mainly every weekend. He became very mean as a drinker. I don't know if he missed having his home to himself or if he really didn't want me anymore but he became really mean. I started to record the way that he would act to me while being drunk so that I could play it back to him on video when he sobered up. I wanted him to see what he becomes. Tony could never watch a video or listen to the recordings. He never wanted to address the elephant in the room but he was a completely different man with a drink in his hand.

I had several conversations with him about how he treats me and I was to the limit and I even had to tell his parents how concerned I was about his health and safety because he didn't believe he had a problem. Arguments with him now would be like swords thrown at each other's head it was so intense & no matter how much I loved him. I could not sit back and listen to the blatant disrespect. It made me actually sit down and try to re-evaluate his childhood, I had questions. I didn't know a man living in a two parent pastoring household had the ability to treat a woman like he often treated me. I wasn't perfect but I bet my life on the fact that I worked hard to not bring to this relationship what I knew from the past.

I held Tony to a higher standard as well, I believed in him with my whole heart. Whenever he wasn't drinking, Tony was the most chill, loving person. It was like two different persons inside one body and it frustrated my soul. I knew he loved me, he showed me. He knew I loved him because I showed him but the enemy was at work in our relationship and it either boiled down to the will of God or

Satan's final demise. I've never dealt with someone with an alcohol abuse issue but with all the issues I've dealt with, with these men out here this was just like every other issue I played around with.

Only this time I should know better, I was delivered from this type of enemy before. I rationalized in a way that made me think about how good he was outside of the liquor and if I could just help him with the drinking we would be okay. I mean he never put his hands on me, right...I would put my hands on him before he would hit me but he was tearing me up emotionally and I wasn't the best mate, Overwhelmed in emotions, I had some choice words for him every time we would argue but overall our relationship wasn't so bad. We had really good times, I mean really great times. We had days where we would go out to the grill and have a feast by the Jacuzzi, we had chill nights by the pool, we had movie dates and shopping sprees. We were best friends, I understood him, the real him and I did my best to cover him from anyone that tried to judge him without knowing who he really was. We had memories for years of good times, some drunk times but good times. I was right by his side. We would post our pictures on social media and when I looked at us together to me we looked like a match made from heaven. We looked good together, this is what god intended, right? He would dress up and put on his suit and tie and myself a dress and heels and we would genuinely smile for the camera but if the lenses had been a magnifying glass, it would've revealed much more.

--If they can't see the beauty in your struggle, they won't know how to love you--

The big blow up happened next. Who knows what the argument was about this time but he called me all kinds of bitches and hoes in front of my daughter mentioning the guys name from my list, I thought we were over this but he asked my daughter if she knew that her mom was a hoe and slept with so and so. Calling me liars and he should've never gotten back with me and so on. It went down in the apartment as I yelled back at him and called him bitches and hoes back. I kept telling him he needs to stop drinking and coming for me but he didn't listen so I gave it to him raw and uncut. I told Tony he needs to focus on his baby boy and stop treating him like an outsider because you have two sons, not one!

I screamed to him about everything I had bottled up inside from how he acted holy and was a selfish disgrace to his two-faced sister. I could not hold it in any longer. I was beyond hurt that I had to go there with him and most of all that my daughter was there to witness it all. I had just escaped the worst of relationships and here I go again.

The apartment he lived in was in his parents name so they got a call from the complex management saying that there was loud noise and arguing going on inside. His parents called us back that night and they could hear us going back and forth over the phone. I was at my wits end with his actions and I didn't care who was on the phone. I found myself using foul language while my bishop listened in on the other end. I was in a terrible mind space and neither one of us could pull ourselves together to just be quiet. Tony said that he wanted me to get out of his place and he wanted me out now. His parents convinced him to let me and my daughter to stay until the morning suggesting that Tony would sleep it off and be ok by the next day but the next day he walked around with an attitude not saying anything to me the whole day through. Even the next day Tony walked around mad at the world, talking to women on the phone at night and still drinking his fifths of liquor. He was so confused he would be asking me "so you ain't gonna cook? Or come get in the bed with me, or fuck you" all in the same breath...

Tony and alcohol simply did not mix. Interesting enough days had gone by and he called his parents telling them that he needed for me to go still. I gave Tony time to sleep it off and think about it fully but he was convinced that he didn't want me there. His parents tried to reason with him but he really didn't listen to anybody unless it was his dad putting his foot down.

My first lady felt sad by it all I believed, she was trying to get me help from some of the churches down there offering to write a letter for me to possibly get some assistance because we were now working and getting established, we didn't want to go back to Michigan but he wanted us out. His mom even told me, "I would tell my two daughters, you don't deserve that and you should leave him" but I didn't listen.

I got on the phone with bishop and he asked me to leave in order to keep the peace, his mom went on to say that they didn't want any problems with the police being called there because their names were on the lease and maybe it was a good idea for me and Shyra to leave. Tony wasn't being friendly about it at all though, he was yelling throwing my things out of the bathroom and telling me to pack up and go all in front of my daughter. I yelled back at him fuck you and your family. I'll leave and I'll leave when I'm done packing. He wanted me to leave right away. My daughter and I began to pack up our things while still arguing with him, my daughter is trying to keep me calm and avoid getting involved in the controversy, Shaking her head in disbelief in the actions of us both. Tony left and went down to his leasing office and changed the locks to the doors. He had thrown my cell phone in the toilet so I went and hid his Rolex watch and some of his clothes from him, in this utility closet because I couldn't believe he damaged my phone but I still couldn't find myself damaging or taking any of his things. We were both operating on a childish level the best thing to do was to just leave and to NEVER come back.

    After changing the locks he sat all of our luggage outside his apartment shoved me out the door and closed the door behind me and my daughter. He locked the door and then drove away in his truck. Leaving my daughter and I curbside of his complex, waiting in the hot sun with all this luggage. If you could see the look on my daughters face, I snapped a picture of her right in that moment to show her how disappointed she was looking. She was let down, she looked angry and she sat there with me waiting quietly on our uber to arrive. My daughter and I both were supposed to be at work at this time so our first stop was in Riverside. We had to go in and suddenly resign with this company and the great people that we were beginning to befriend.

    Our uber driver was so nice after one stop and hearing us talk amongst ourselves about what happened, he chimed in to say he just wanted to be a blessing to us. He knew that our flight wasn't until later that evening and we had time so he took the rest of his work day off and took me and my daughter out to eat at a chicken spot. He asked "why would your boyfriend do ya'll like that?" and all I could blame it on was his drinking. Our uber driver stopped the meter long ago because he didn't want us to incur anymore charges but he encouraged us and looked out for us and he took us to the airport free of charge. We still had a couple of hours before our flight so my daughter wanted to cheer me up, she said "mom, come with me let's get us some massages while we wait, you deserve it." My daughter paid for me a massage as we waited for our flight to board. We both knew of Tony's deep rooted issues but we were still shocked and heart-broken that we both decided to give him a chance and his actions towards us was everything except Godly. I no longer felt safe with this man and I didn't know what I did to him to deserve such disrespect.

My family was also disturbed by the whole thing, my mom especially very hurt by the way things were handled for the second time and with her grandbaby being involved. There was no sugar coating the way that she felt about Tony going forward. Needless to say I was back at home with my parents, wasted money, wasted my time and I hurt my family again but for some reason I felt like I was right where God wanted me to be. I started back focusing on my organization and I had a ton of support and love throughout this journey. There was still purpose for my life and God was still speaking to me. The enemy would have loved for me to believe that healing wasn't possible for me or that it was my actions that caused men to be the way that they were towards me but although I knew I wasn't completely innocent, I would never forsake the authenticity of me. I knew who I was and who I was in Christ. It was crucial that I didn't become emotionally numb because I had swallowed too much at once. So I began to take my time with myself.

When you have been praying for someone and you are a child of God. It is hard to talk bad about that person, either you believe in them or you don't. I prayed hard for Tony, it reminded me of how hard I use to go for my ex-husband and I just knew this would someday be my husband so that's why I fought harder and didn't give up so easily, I still didn't want to end things with this man after all of that. My heart was completely tied in to his existence but it was space that he needed so I gave him that. I started to learn of myself, my triggers & my choices. Tony and I didn't talk for weeks in fact he had blocked me from social media and from calling him so I wasn't able to contact him if I wanted to. We played the block game heavy. I would block him from calling me and he would block me from calling him, silly games.

One day I got a text from him that opened me back up emotionally. I felt my life was falling to pieces and our sacred intimate connection was nearly destroyed. Of course we both missed each other but yet he would still come in town and pretend I didn't exist. He used this time to play around and talk to different girls from his past while I was praying and fasting about our relationship. This is why God spoke to me concerning us often and sent prophets my way to speak to me also because I stayed in communication with him about us. I would talk to his mom and she would advise me to continue praying and fasting, "Tony will come around don't worry about him. Just keep looking good and doing you, trust me, I know my son." Would be her advice, I was back in a toxic relationship after I had been renewed.

With all the things that Tony would do negatively to hurt our relationship he put more of an effort in to make things better and that's what I respected about him. I paid more attention to his efforts than his actual execution but he did try to correct his wrongs, he did. It was just a matter of how do we stop the wrong from re-occurring. As a Christian this should've been easy but it wasn't.

--Confidence in a disloyal man in time of trouble is like a broken tooth, and a foot out of joint, Proverbs 25:19--

Life Lesson *12* – Cycles & Curses can be broken

This might seem too crazy to comprehend for most but Tony made his way back around as my friend and my man. After putting both me and my daughter out on the curb miles away from home where we knew no one, I forgave him. I loved him still. I knew who he was outside of his addiction and that's what gave me the confidence I needed. It was hard for me to convince others of that because I couldn't tell everyone he abused alcohol, it wasn't everybody's business. My daughter understood and that's what mattered to me most. She allowed me to make my own decision concerning getting back with him.

Meanwhile Tony's after school program wasn't doing so good now and that was his main source of income. Tony was now forced to make a decision and it resulted in him coming back to Detroit. He did as best he could to feel comfortable living here again and adapting to this new life being stripped of his independence so to speak but he wasn't feeling it at first. His goal was to get back to Cali ASAP but if anybody knew how difficult it was to start completely over in life, it was me. After leaving California, I worked two jobs to save up extra money to get my life, peace and sanity back. I got approved for an apartment which I thought would never happen with my prior eviction but as Tony was moving in with his parents, I was moving into my new apartment so we were both in transition. I hadn't been to church in a month or so because my motor blew on my truck, I even had faith enough to go to the dealership and was approved for a newer vehicle too. God started blessing me back to back to back. I felt on track and with my man being here now, I felt we would do much better in the city together as a couple. I knew some things had humbled Tony because back in Cali everything was about him, what belonged to him and what he could do. He was definitely not use to sharing with anyone. I knew not to ever make him feel the way he made me feel when he put me out. In fact the tables had turned full circle he could no longer take away from me because God had blessed me despite my disobedience to move there in the first place. He allowed me to obtain things for myself and my daughter on our own. I was careful to not be selfish with anything but grateful for everything. I wanted to show Tony the qualities I thought he was missing, our relationship was missing. Those things that were taught to me outside of the church, the principles I valued in life.

    We were doing good for a nice little while until one night after visiting Tony at his parents. He invited me back over the next day to celebrate the holiday with him. I had to work but I told him I would try and stop by. I ended up getting off work a little early that night, I waitressed at a restaurant and we were slow that night so I called him and told him that I would be getting changed to come over. After I got off and went home to get changed, I called Tony & he didn't answer. I knew he was right at his parent's house and maybe he didn't have his phone near him so I continued to call and instead of the phone ringing this time, it went to voice mail. Tony was ignoring my calls and why would he do this? We weren't even beefing! We're good right now, what's really going on, I thought to myself.

    I texted Tony "remember you invited me over?" and no reply. Yes I took it upon myself to still go over to his parent's, I did not wait on his reply. My eyes have witnessed yet again... I go over there to find Tony cuddled up in the backyard with one of his ex's. I walked closer in disbelief to see if my eyes were deceiving me and before I knew it, I crept up from behind them and slapped him upside the back of his head without notice "what are you doing and who is this?" Tony sat there astonished for a second and after realizing it was me he started to verbally bash me like he normally does. It was apparent that he had been drinking too much. His sister got involved, saying "Tony ain't got no woman" and blah blah blah. I wasn't even paying her no attention, it was clear to me already the type of person she was. My first lady came out and asked to speak with me out front away from everyone. Tony continued to curse me and talk down at me in front of everyone, "Tell that bitch to leave" he says. My first lady asked Tony and his sister to both be quiet as she talked to her spiritual daughter (trying to diffuse things) and his sister blurts out "Spiritual daughter haha, She ain't been to church in I don't know how long." My first lady tried to explain to his big mouth sister that I was just there with Tony the night before but She was talking more crap than him per usual. Listening to the both, it became me arguing at them and them at me in front of this ex-chick. I strived to be respectful in front of my first lady and I did just as she said when she asked me to leave and I left. If I would have had my way, I wouldn't have left without punching a few people.

I would have never expected Tony to play me in front of any woman and to disrespect me in front of everyone the way that he did. Tony barely respected his mother when he drank so I don't know why I expected anything different. He was just a mean drunk at times.

I left and he carried on with his fling or whatever for a couple days. He spent the rest of that day and the next day with this girl and started posting her on his instagram story while they hung out. If he wanted to get my attention somehow, he sure did. It became more than drinking, I now questioned his faithfulness but long story short he was able to apologize and plead his way back in to my life yet again, yes even after all of that. The drinking, well it didn't get any better, it got worst but I clung on to all his promises.

Tony started to be at my apartment with me mostly. He hadn't moved in but he was there day and night. He would drink liquor in the morning for breakfast lunch and dinner. I was extremely concerned. I knew that he would eventually hurt himself or someone else because he would do random things like go to the car to drive away or start walking off. I've had to go and get him from bars because he was slumped over in public. I've had to hide his car keys from him, poured out fifths of liquor while he went to sleep and lord knows I've prayed my lips blue. I would pray & put anointed oil on his forehead, his mouth and his hands as he slept, speaking to his spirit when he would awake constantly trying to speak to the king in him and the rest of the time was just arguments about the drinking or anything.

I believed I finally had found the man that I loved and wanted to spend the rest of my life with and nothing was standing in our way but this demon called alcohol. I called his parents often to tell them just how he was acting. I felt like I would be responsible if anything were to happen to him. I would often reach out to them in despair and often times his mom would reach out to me just to make sure he was doing okay. I realized they had a lot going on with the ministry but somehow Tony had become a priority to me instead of them. I would call his mom only about his progress or the lack thereof. Sometimes he would be so out of control that we would have to get bishop involved. I didn't know what else to do, I didn't want to handle him like I did every other man but at times I was left no choice, I knew defense well. I did not like to go there with him but this relationship was beginning to remind me of the past and I thought I was with a totally different man than I've ever been with before. Tony would get drunk and want to attend worship with alcohol literally seeping through his pours. He insisted on going to church one Sunday morning after a night of extreme alcohol intake. He had the shakes the whole night through and he was not okay but you couldn't tell him nothing so off to church we went. As soon as service started, he began to throw up liquid and blood. He hadn't eaten a full meal in a few days and his eyes were a yellowish tent, he nearly passed out. The ambulance had to be called and all the elders and ministers came rushing to lay hands on him praying this 'sickness" away but I had been praying about this demon for a long time so I tried to make sure no one got close enough to find out what the real sickness was. I sat at the hospital with him for two days and after many tests and him sobering up, they discharged him.

    Tony promised me he would never drink again. The doctor told him that if he continued on this path he would surely die. He chose to sober up and get it together. Tony could do whatever he put his mind to. He could be a very disciplined person whenever he focused his mind to do something but that only worked for so long and he was right back with the bottle.

    I had become the typical church person. Hide your pains and you don't address the real issue because privately God will get you through it and that's how I continued on. If I could get him out of church in time to not be noticed by others that's what I did because it could be embarrassing as well. This was my future husband in my mind and he needed me as much as I needed him so I had his back through it all. Nobody in that church was perfect, trust me and I knew for sure his heart towards God is the most genuine I've seen so who cares what they had to say honestly. I just got tired of the façade and I wanted real deliverance and healing to take place for the both of us. We were too busy with the typical counterfeit approach. God wanted our hearts pure and confessional. God could've have fixed this. Instead I spent time trusting in his parents to help me, help him not knowing they were agitated by me and I was a bother to them with the constant communication of our shortcomings. I couldn't win for losing in love.

Tony had later been arrested for his 2nd DUI. He was found passed out in the middle of 696 highway. Tony would say that he was conscious enough and he pulled over to get some rest because he got tired but the police report tells a different story either way this was the awakening that we needed. Tony drank clean up unto his court day, completely giving up and he even said to me if he went to jail, so be it. It was as if he stopped caring. I was scared for his life because he was giving up. How is it that the man that was so much life for me can struggle in this way.

He was at the lowest point that I had ever seen him before. He allowed life circumstances to weigh him down. He was unable to see his first born but he had grown much closer to his youngest son, we both did. That kid was so amazing to me. I grew to love his son so much. I know Tony wasn't working but he was always able to get money so it wasn't clear what plagued him but it was clear that Tony was depressed and he would often tell me I drink because I like to and because I want to. He was the 4 S's selfish, stubborn, stingy and spoiled. He had an easy $50 or more per day drinking habit with no serious income, how is this possible? He had access to his dad's bank account and no one wanted to take away his privilege to spend how he wanted to even if it was on alcohol.

Bishop would have talks with him but his response was always "We're praying about it and he'll be okay." I found out exactly why he responded this way, this was inherited behavior that he passed down to his son. Bishop was no stranger to alcohol either so he dealt with Tony with a remorseful kind of love. I wasn't raised quite like that, we prayed about things but my mother was an alpha woman. She held no bars when it came to the love she had for us. Likewise, I was in his face about change. I wasn't too sure that he would be okay...I had a different way of expressing my love and concern. I didn't want to bury my man and I made sure he understood just that. Tony probably didn't like that about me but he knew I meant him no harm in my approach.

Tony was now facing 2 years in jail because of his drinking and I know my man, He was not built for nobody's jail cell. It wouldn't have been such a bad idea, otherwise. I wanted what would work but I did not want him to be in jail, I prayed hard about it but Gods will be done to clean this up because I had been dealing with this for way too long.

There is always, always a ram in the bush, thank the lord because there was this sobriety program that his lawyer mentioned and we were able to get his attorney to go before the judge to ask if he would allow him to enroll in this program. It seemed like just the type of assistance he needed. The attorney didn't think it would work but with the favor of God he had a limited amount of time to get processed and enrolled and pay off some fines and they would allow him to be enrolled, What a blessing!

Tony began the program and sobered up immediately. It was like honey from a honey comb the way I felt having all of him, in his right mind. He was finally focused enough to get back focused. We spent all of our days together and we started a different approach. We both had our own personal relationship with God and although we would pray together we didn't include God in on our relationship like we should have. We implemented fasting and more communing with God into our daily routine so that we could be strengthened in the lord. We read our bibles and we talked about a more promising future together.

We made plans to look for another place since a year had gone by and I no longer wanted to be in that apartment so we both were looking at places to move to, finally Tony comes home one day and says "Babe, I found an apartment complex you would like, it's nice lets go by and look at it" and so we did. I set up the appointment for us to look at it and this would be our fresh new start, a beautiful space and not too expensive. We prayed and filled out the application together but the application was denied. I said to Tony, "since you're still working on your credit build, let's try it again but with just me applying this time and see what happens" and so I applied by myself and I was approved. We were happy about the move. We slowly started packing and we were out with the old and in with the new in no time. Tony had taken care of all the moving needs and made it struggle free for me and my daughter. We didn't have to lift a finger, this is what it felt like having a whole man around. He always took the initiative to do what he needed to do and I appreciated him for that. Alcohol to the side this was the man of my dreams.

--I don't want to hear your opinion about someone I love unless you have the same love for them that I do—My King!

We made our new place our new home, it had been over four years of us going back and forth in this relationship and finally we were solid and where we needed to be. Tony assured me that he wanted to fully commit to me. With all the time that had gone by of course my family forgave him for his wrong doings well my mom a little bit but they loved me so much that they only wanted to see me happy and if that meant, Tony...They love, who I love. Tony and I have always talked of marriage, this was nothing new. If it wasn't for all the hiccups and issues we had down the road. We probably would have been tied the knot but we were giving each other a chance to become better and do better for one another because we both had concerns to be honest and God knows I wasn't perfect either I violated his privacy in many ways, so many times...checking his phone when he would be drunk and couldn't hold water about all the disrespect I saw, I would cause all kinds of havoc. I would hit Tony many times right where he stood because he could be such an asshole in the way that he handled me sometimes. I for sure gave him a run for his money concerning me and my feelings but this sobriety program was working well for us. He was a willing vessel and that's how I knew he would succeed at most anything.

Despite our past and our toxicities Tony asked me for my hand in marriage one day. He and my daughter got all my family and close friends together at our family and friends day service at church and he surprised my socks off when he took the microphone and asked me to be his wife. I had some clues but he did a real good job hiding all of that from me, I'm Miss investigative queen. Apparently my daughter and Tony had this ring picked out for months and he was just waiting on the perfect time to propose. I could say I was the happiest in that moment. I felt a release in my prayers and a shifting in our lives. I thought it would be for the better but there was something that kept dividing us. All I wanted was for my man to sober up and I figured after we got this drinking behind us. We would be the perfect couple in all of our imperfections, I mean perfect for each other. There are no perfect couples but we were working US out. However with his sobriety I noticed that certain traits and characteristics that I would once blame on the alcohol did not go away. I had only had my ring on my finger one month before he was throwing it up in my face and making me feel unworthy to be wearing it. He always demanded certain things and with my background of abuse it just wasn't rubbing me the right way. I was advocating for domestic abuse and I would talk to these women and I would teach them the red flags and I would question the way I was being treated at home every time. I knew he had some toxic ways, hell I did too but I began to grow and learn and heal and it showed in the way that I was changing. I believe when we first got together it was a trauma bonding, one had to heal the other but that was no longer bonding us together. It was clear that we needed to make some changes but guess what with God nothing is impossible so let's work a little more. That was always our stance.

    I treated Tony like the man of the house, like my king at least I thought I did. I have not one problem with submitting to a man that I trust is being led by God and I knew Tony consulted with God concerning us so I was in good hands but the disrespect kept showing up. I couldn't explain that, It seemed we argued about anything. We would get off track and get right back on track and repeat. Because we both know God we would quickly get it together but the reoccurrence was way too often. It was like misery on some of our days and I just didn't want to settle in this way. The more I was asked to speak at seminars or events on the signs of unhealthy relationships with my organization, the more I questioned the stability of my own. It strengthened me to help strengthen others but I was giving advice that I wasn't taking myself. I knew what was acceptable and what was not and the more I stood up for myself and set boundaries in regards to what I would like or not, the more Tony puffed up at me and became a shell. If ever we were at odds Tony would ask for his ring back automatically. If I had to speak in public, he would give it back to me so that people wouldn't notice. I got tired of that, I didn't feel appreciated at all. I worked full time, paid most the bills as he saved for our wedding or whatever but I cooked twice a day for my man and I even gave his not so cute feet pedicures and rubbed him down if ever he was distressed. I gave him the very best parts of me, sex was never an issue but what I could not allow was a sober Tony to continue to talk to me or treat me any kind of way. You don't always have to be a cheater to ruin things. I had no signs of other women at this point in time but he was inconsiderate, lacked empathy, had poor communication skills and was harboring his emotions.

I asked Tony to leave the apartment we shared because I felt we needed a break to appreciate each other more and to take some time to re-evaluate our position in each other's lives. We were still very much engaged, there was no reason why we couldn't communicate about everything even in separating, it was the mature thing to do but Tony says you wanted space, I gave you space and that's all that matters. I asked him to meet me so that we could take a walk, this was my attempt to get my fiancé's understanding and to cry out about the way that he treats me for the last time and instead of him listening to my feelings he made excuses for his actions and disregarded them. That night ended in argument.

He began to stay away from home all day and night now and when he came back he would go straight in another room. He never did this when weren't engaged and he had taken my ring again, He stopped answering my calls when he would leave and would tell me that he was working and couldn't answer. I felt avoided and on top of that he started making decisions without me that would hurt my feelings. When Tony took the blanket from me one night and told me it was his blanket and to get my own, that was my final straw. I slept on the couch that night, my daughter said to me "Momma you can come sleep with me in my bed" but I told her No, I just wanted to cry to myself especially after hearing my daughter say "Mom, I know your worth more than you do."

Seemed as though whatever he could do to feel superior, he was doing it. That night I told him he was acting like a bitch and the whole world stopped because we both agreed there would be no more name calling ever again. We did that enough. If I say you're acting like a bitch, is that really calling you one? I knew what I was doing and it was dead wrong but you ever met someone that could do and say whatever they wanted to but the moment you bark back, You're totally out of order and in fact it's all about what you've done now. You're the one with the problem and now they're the victim. He had some narcissistic ways for sure. Tony never valued me as his queen in its fullest essence, he just wanted to be recognized as king but the story of king and queen as I knew it works both ways and if we were going to continue to blatantly disrespect one another than I wanted him gone. I wanted him out of our apartment. I did not want to deal with a man like that for the rest of my life. I was tired of my daughter seeing us bicker and argue. I put her through enough, enough damage has been done. I begged this man to please go to counseling with me, I still wanted to make us work. I wanted to talk with a qualified professional. I had been through a lot, in my life alone and I have never been pulled to the side and counseled by spiritual figures or even us together as a couple. Tony ego deemed it a waste of money and used the excuse of others knowing our business. I was ready to expose the enemy for our marriage sake but he wouldn't go. I had been through hell and back in my last relationship and Tony knew of it all. He was simply incapable of keeping true to what he promised because he was hurting too and that I didn't know. His efforts became zero to none. I texted his family and I said he needs to leave I've tried all I can try and I was adamant because I was done.

He had taken his ring back for the 3rd and final time within only 3 months. He even said "I should've never asked you to marry me."

    I had taken away his key to the apartment and he was coming and going as he pleased. There was nothing left but yet I still hoped that this would get his attention. Instead it did the exact opposite. I left for work the next day and Tony with the help of his family had arranged for all of his things to be packed up and delivered to his parents and that included all things. This man took everything he bought in the house down to the mount on the wall, who takes a mount with no TV, I mean he had uninstalled everything he put together, shower head, night lights. He even threw my unclean panties on the floor to take the dirty clothes basket that he had purchased. He was clearly not interested in coming back and my attempt to open his eyes, epic fail. He had been influenced by his loved ones and his own ego and this was somehow all of my fault. I put him out and you don't put the king out, not Tony.

Well that afternoon after work. I came home to empty spaces in my apartment, no sign of Tony at all and he wouldn't even answer my calls. I looked at my daughter and I cried. I meant every word I said but I didn't mean every single word I said. Tony immediately started moving like a single man seeking attention from any and everyone as soon as the very next day. He had his birthday dinner without me, I didn't know the location and he started making a huge scene on social media for everyone to notice that we were no longer together. I would watch his page as he and some family members talked slick about me and played me like I hadn't been good to him all these years. I sacrificed so much in our relationship and watching him rant and rave for the world to see was like a slap in my face. I realized you have to evaluate a person's maturity, morals and growth because you're not just dating their physical image and Tony was all about an image. He had to portray a certain image and in his story, he's never the bad guy. No matter what I said he insists that it never happened that way!

It had become so much that I couldn't and wouldn't respond back because he was clearly choosing his path and if it was that easy for him to replace me then we had nothing to begin with. What was even scarier is that I was so hurt behind our break up and the embarrassment of it all that I couldn't eat, sleep or focus at work. I lost 15 pounds easily. I had to take a leave of absence, I went to the doctor's office one day and was diagnosed with depression and anxiety and prescribed sleeping pills just to help me get through the night. I didn't know what to do my whole world had turned upside down.

Tony was going on dates with women and posting about it making statuses about how he's now single and yet he was still reaching out to me late at night and texting me about us fixing things. He was now pretending to be done with me publicly but privately he was still coming to the apartment and staying the night and taking me out and sleeping with me. I was in a state of mental anguish. I thought I would lose my mind if I wasn't with him and I did, I was losing control. I tried to do as instructed and be still but this shattered all that I believed in. It was betrayal to me and I was allowing him to do so because I felt guilty about telling him to leave or putting him out as he says. Somehow I thought we were still salvageable.

He happened to complete and graduate from his sobriety program during our separation and I met him at the courthouse to show him how proud of him I was. We both fought that demon together and it was all glory to God that the curse had been broken off his life. No matter what was going on with us at the time it was imperative that I be there. I wanted to be there and I even took him out to dinner afterwards to celebrate. He deserved to be celebrated for this because I witnessed his struggle and I was so Godly proud of him for 2 years of being sober.

Things were quite different for us but I knew for sure things had changed when his dad called him and asked him where he was and he responded by saying "I'm over a friend's house" but he was lying right next to me. I was now a secret to everyone and I didn't like that. I felt like the side chick at this point while he went around exploring. I stayed as quiet as my maturity would allow with all the rumors that I heard because to me, we were planning on getting back together.

That's what we discussed when we were together but Tony manipulated the situation well. I put up a fight to save our relationship just like I fought throughout it to keep it but that wasn't enough. He was just waiting for the right person to come along that gave him the attention he desired so that he could use that as fuel to move on and be happy and that's what he did. We lost complete contact, for a while by the end August, we talked again last in May and by next July he was living with another woman, in love and had asked her to be his wife. Yikes but this was the way that God intended so I fought no more. Our separation didn't end with integrity like two Christian adults that once loved each other but it was distasteful in my eyes.

I had no more prayers to pray concerning us. I had no more rationalizing to do. I had no choice but to move on and focus on me. You'd be surprised how many blessings start to find their way to you when you decide to detach yourself from things or people that aren't a part of your destiny. Although people will recognize your confusion and pain, no one really knew the state of insanity I was in. God isolated me from everyone and like the potter that he is, he worked on my strength and my mind day in and day out, building me back up. He was healing me from the inside and stretching me for a higher level of growth. I could feel every stitch to the touch. I didn't know that breaking up with him meant that I no longer had spiritual parents either but they cut me off completely and that broke my heart. I couldn't believe I had served at a ministry that didn't have leaders that were willing to at least call and check on me. I retreated to PTSD and re-victimization all over again but God used the betrayal to teach me more about him and the power of his might. The rejection that I endured taught me a very valuable lesson. People don't let you down you just hold them up too high because inside of every person you know, there's really a person you don't know. I heard a great woman say it best...You don't tell people how to love, you get to experience their type of love and if it's not the kind of love that you desire you get to choose whether or not you want to participate in it. So after all of that, God brought me out. I exhale knowing that what is meant to be, will be. I am unapologetically healed and thriving because God has resuscitated me for what's ahead. It was not easy for me to digest that I got myself back in the same boat but I started to pay attention to my patterns. I thought my last relationship was the best option for me. He wasn't a drug dealer like the rest, he read the bible with me and we prayed together but although he treated me better than everyone else, he still wasn't treating me the way that I deserved to be treated. Look at what I had to compare him to. Tony hurt me more than the man that shot me multiple times while my back was turned because I expected that from Chuck. I never imagined Tony would learn of me and then turn around and try to break me. I found a worth in God that didn't match our love story and for once in my life I made the decision to stand up as a woman and honor the boundaries in which I had set for myself. The problem is the men in my life never saw the storm coming. People will continue to do to you what you allow them to. I am now in the best place in my life although it is the most uncomfortable. I have no desire to be accompanied by just any man no matter what he looks like or can provide. God has created something special inside of me and it has nothing to do with a man.

The best for me is yet to come, in life and in love. . Journey with me through my unknown future as it relates to love.

Life Lesson 13 - Take a look back, then look forward & love intentionally, still.

It all starts to make sense, I finally decided to do the work necessary to figure out how I became the type of individual that I once was. I had to reach deep, deeper than my very first relationship with an abusive guy at just 16 years old. I had to look back even further to grasp an understanding of why I would ever be attracted to someone that could treat me like less than gum on the bottom of a shoe. I was on a mission to get the answers that would reveal to me my lowest self. I needed to address the low me in order to conquer the insane parts of me so that I could revert to becoming my highest self. The desire to become was eating away at me by day and keeping me up by night. There was an urgency to unveil all the filthy things about me that didn't make me so proud. This plagued at me like a whining baby that yearns milk from its mommy. I was restless, tired and afraid but with resuscitation came a determination to discover my healing once and for all. I've learned a lot about myself during this process of healing and one thing that stuck out like a sore thumb is that when I was just two years old, my father was taken away from me. I never got a chance to meet my daddy. He got into an argument with his sister's boyfriend, at his sister's house and her boyfriend stabbed my dad several times in the back and then hit him in the head with a baseball bat. I imagined my wounded father crawling to the busy street of Van Dyke in desperate need of help from anyone as the only person that could've helped him turned her back and walked away. He later died from those wounds and there it was, the curse of another fatherless female child. You ever heard the saying "you can't miss what you've never had." I believed this for a long time especially because I had the best step-father this world could offer me, he came into my life at 5 years old and he has been wonderful to my mom and all three of her children. Reality would set in and tell me that there was something missing in me and I would have to challenge that cliché now. Subconsciously I missed what I never had, what was supposed to be a part of me. I've seen his face on pictures. I've heard his voice on cassette tapes. I've met his family (my family) and I've always missed him. That was my daddy! Flesh of my flesh, blood of my blood and it hurts that I don't remember a single moment with him, just years on top of years without him.

When a baby is 2 years of age they have officially reached toddlerhood. Instead of learning my dad, I was learning to live without him. At an age where you develop your motor and social skills, I had an added disposition of separation anxiety that left a stain on me. It showed up later in life in many ways and in several relationships as if I was a toddler again. The feelings of desperation and habits of dysfunction that I knew early on was not limited to but contributed to the absence of my father. Generational Curses and my environment played its part as well but all of these issues kept me in a struggle my entire life and held me captive. I was not at peace for a very long time and I knew nothing about real freedom. I wanted to control everything and everybody that appeared to threaten me or hurt me in anyway as a way of protection. I wanted to prevent the hurt, address the pain and return to the neglect all at the same time. I showed up in battles as someone else because I had been dehumanized, I forgot who I was. I developed a fear of losing and instead I was willing to be demeaned and overlooked by the men that I loved. I became so passionate about love that at times I was halfhearted. The enemy used the men in my life to create a false reality about me to get me to believe that I was unworthy and at the same time desperate for love but God intervenes. His presence in my life is a constant reminder that he would never leave me nor forsake me even when others have.

In this book, I have given you the real life experiences that I've gone through in several different relationships. You see that my relationships were back to back without taking the necessary time to heal my heart and rid myself of all of the negativity that was created around me. I wish I could have explained more in grave detail all the damage that was done as a result of unhealthy love but I have done my best to summarize certain situations to give you an idea of how these relationships have landed me where I am today, here writing to you. I take full responsibility for the way that I presented my love in these relationships and I wish that I could have discerned better but I had a lot of growing to do. I would love for one to remember me simply as the loving, passionate, and giving individual that I am but the truth is we all have our issues and none of us are perfect.

    These men that you have read about at one point in my life meant a lot to me and some still do. I'm happy to say that Rico has been granted a rehearing with the Supreme Court after 15 years of imprisonment, he is finally on the path to justice and a grand victory in Jesus name. I have no resentment or ill will with any of my exes. My only goal is to tell my truth and help prevent others from being caught up in the web of toxicity. Whether it be by way of your environment, your nature or your DNA. Nothing will change if you don't acknowledge your faults and apply certain principles to your life, which is why I've self examined myself and spent more time with myself and learned more of me. What triggers me and what's not safe for me. It's important that you have that mirror to look into, the kind that talks back truth and affirmation.

    We must learn to love ourselves and take good care of ourselves and not self-betray. It is not okay to stick around to find out if someone is who you would want them to be. When someone shows you who they are, please believe them. As a woman there is a tendency to want to help, nurture and shape our boys into men but that is simply not our responsibility. Men lead, not the other way around and whether it's fixing a plumbing issue or negotiating a business deal, A woman needs to see her man execute and deliver, which also means we have to allow a man to be a man.

    Some of us are so use to handling our own business that we step on the toes of real men when they do show up and likewise some men are head driven and stuck in the late 1800's where women never had a voice. Submission is easy and should never be forced but It is also your responsibility as a person to protect yourself from anything that threatens your happiness and throws you off balance. You do not owe sympathy or consideration to any person that has walked all over you. You simply need to see the good in goodbye and move on because disrespect can be an accurate boomerang.

    We must learn to channel our emotions. Women live a great deal by our feelings and it seems to be the believer's number one enemy. To conquer this it requires a level of stretching that you can't even prepare for. You will fail miserably in almost everything you do if you do not learn to control yourself. Often times in the church we are taught tolerance and intolerance rather than good and evil and what we end up with is a tolerance of evil.

Feelings of jealousy, insecurities, playing detective and disliking people you've never met are all normal feelings when your partner has manufactured paranoia, competition and drama in your life. Don't give in to those that label you "the crazy girl" no one has the right to judge the way you respond to the trauma that was given to you. You have the right however to turn that trauma into a testimony for the good. Anything that has power over you is teaching you how to get your power back. The good news is that with time and diligence feelings can be trained to come under the leadership of the spirit. Often times we give expression to things of the flesh but we do have a choice to not feed into fleshly responses. We have two choices. We can demonstrate Gods word or we can express the enemy's work. Whose child are you?

Everyone sees life from their side of the fence. Don't make everything you don't like about a person, a character flaw. And let's not judge emotions that we are uninformed about. Your responses could be normal reactions to abnormal events. Everyone has gone through their own experiences and issues and it has a direct impact on their thoughts and actions.

An undisciplined person can be wild and uncontrollable, always wanting to do his or her own thing but God desires for us to put on his mindset and that's why we need the help of the holy spirit. We must learn discipline and we must take responsibility for what we produce. We are no longer children not knowing right from wrong. There is a correct way to love someone and God has given us the perfect example of this. It is no longer love if mutual respect doesn't exist. Let's not give power to the adversary and pretend to ignore this fact. We have to respect one another, our boundaries and our healing process.

People, if we are not speaking the language of God we need to close our mouths. Ignore the if's and the but's and make a decision based on the facts and learn to differentiate between the sound of your intuition guiding you and your trauma misleading you. Use the knowledge that you have right now and don't be afraid to stand behind your decision. Create and honor the boundaries that you have set for yourself, Step into your power by reminding yourself of what you've been able to overcome already. Open your heart to the possibility of genuine love. It takes more courage to surrender to love than to become emotionally numb. Be of good courage and God will strengthen your heart.

I know they hurt you, I know you didn't deserve it, I know you were taken advantage of but this healing is for YOU not them. The most damaged people feel every little bitty thing and we struggle between an authentic life and a falsified energy but God's promises are true, He won't leave you comfortless.

Directly after experiencing any trauma is going to be the most critical time in your life. It is as equally important the kind of people you surround yourself with, for you need a safe space to process your emotions. Seek professional counseling and don't feel like you're difficult or uneasy to love. You are stronger when you wake up with the confidence to love another day. Pain is treacherous but purpose will always out wrestle pain. The pain won't always last but we must never forget what it has taught us. Don't be bullied by your past, your future looks much better when you believe. As a believer I know that truth and mercy will always bless those who have endured life's toughest battles. Meditate and restore yourself back to being whole and trusting in God the most high.

Most importantly HEAL, healing is yours for the taking and don't let anyone take that promise from you. With healing you will be lonely with growing you will be uncomfortable but you will be better in time. The closer you get to your healing expect less and less people to be there at the top of the mountain to help you celebrate. That's okay, you continue to journey with Grace. Make peace with your past and FORGIVE everyone that has ever hurt you. It is your responsibility to forgive, God gave the command. That is how you get your peace back and become emotionally intelligent. Forgiveness opens a pathway to a new place of endless possibilities. There's this cliché floating around, that black women have attitudes. I don't feed into that energy because I see many black women who were left unprotected and hurt. No matter your race or background Kings don't stop protecting your queens, we need you.

I have opened up and I have been transparent about my most personal relationships and I have exposed anything that the enemy could try to use against me but one thing I should mention is my biggest faults. I thought I could chase behind a man and make him be to me what he promised me to be in the beginning but the fact of the matter is, people are allowed to change their minds! It is not becoming for a woman to show any man that their vulnerable and hopeless without him. In all of my relationships you will see some type of intrusive behavior; showing up unannounced, snooping, assuming things will happen without clarifying it first and bringing up topics that aren't ready to be discussed. If a man wants to mislead, manipulate, cheat or beat you, that is his choice and for every choice there are his consequences to deal with. Not only was I intrusive but I had a daughter watching me through it all. The decisions that I made could have affected the way she feels about men or relationships today. She did not deserve to see unhealthy love within our household. It was my responsibility to cover her and guard her eyes and her ears from all that was damaging and dangerous. I was a teenage mom so I grew up with my daughter but that is no excuse for the lack of emotional literacy that she needed that I didn't provide. I had a lot of making up to do and I did a lot of healing so that my daughter could live freely outside of the cycle that I broke for us. I am very blessed that my daughter is strong-minded and knows how to think, I taught her to think for herself because I realized that at times, my thinking was unstable. Self-Care is putting your children first, as parents we must do what's best for our children and not be neglectful.

God will take care of the broken hearted, that's a promise! And you don't have to be the cause of something, you also don't want to be the effect. I wanted RESPECT above everything and If it's respect that you desire more than anything, more than attention, more than love then you MUST know that respect is freely given. I spoke to my ex-Ken recently and I asked him how is it that we were so toxic, when we loved each other so much and he said to me "No matter what I did, you would always take me back and that made us toxic." He said that he never expected to look around one day and I would be gone. He thought he would never lose me so he kept on abusing me. Take your power back! We hear it all the time we teach people how to treat us.

For those of you that are in abusive relationships and are struggling with what choice to make. Simply wake up and decide you don't want to feel this way again and just like that, change it! If you can imagine something better for yourself, you have the ability to create it and if you can't see pass the relationship right now, its okay... continue to pray and work on yourself because once you change your mind, the circumstances around you will change as well. Don't worry about time, concentrate on impact. You will be forever changed and there is no time frame on that. Learn yourself, who you are and what you want in life. Spend time with God and in self-reflection, you will find the answers that you need.

I have been honest in my truth while trying to be gentle in the way that I presented my truth so that others involved aren't hurt. For once in my life I consciously enjoy who I am, who I've become on purpose. I've learned to survive because I've committed myself to mastering every area of life. Some won't recognize me anymore and I'll be happy to reintroduce myself to them. I use to believe that I couldn't be healed because I was still triggered or afraid but now I know that healing is not perfection. I've learned self care in the way of addressing my own problematic behaviors and thoughts and I learned how to do the necessary work to become emotionally wise.

I heard a doctor say that research shows that when a person has a reaction to something there's a 90 second chemical process that happens in the body; after that, any remaining emotional response is just the person choosing to stay in that emotional loop. Remember it's often the story that we create from those emotions that stick with us. I believe that 10% of conflicts are due to differences in opinions. 90% are due to the wrong tone of voice. There is a way to stand up for yourself and not be argumentative. Reframe how you state your feelings mood and emotions, this will create space for growth and exploration. Prayer and meditation have helped restore my energy. If I could be honest I didn't even want to remember the abuse so to talk about it over and over again was some form of abuse all over again but what I didn't realize is that while I spoke to others, I began to heal inwardly. I've given myself new positive habits and I take things day by day. I had something to prove to myself and I'm here to share the memo. I am not who I used to be, you too can escape the evils set out to steal and control your life by simply renewing your mind daily and making decisions that lead to the path you want in life. All things broken can be mended with good intention.

I pray that this book was able to reach the hands of the people who need it the most, to spark the brain for change and touch the heart for healing.

Stepping into my boldness... I decree and I declare to every person reading this book ...That Domestic Abuse, Domestic Violence, Unhealthy & Toxic Relationships will no longer be a part of your life, it shall be a thing of the past for you. No longer shall you be bound by the dysfunctions of inappropriate love. I break the curse off of your life as you read and agree with me today, that YOU WILL experience true love and you will give true love to all that you get the opportunity to love in this lifetime. Be free from every hurt and fear so that you make room for what's to come, you deserve the very best in love no matter what your past looks like. I bind up abuse of any kind and I loose peace and restoration to your life. I pray in Jesus Holy name -Shalom-Amen!

Get Help…..

If you or someone you know is being abused mentally, physically, verbally or sexually please contact your local police department or dial 911.

There is additional help and support at **The National Domestic Violence Hotline** 1-800-799-SAFE (7233) or TTY 1-800-787-3224. Highly trained advocates are available 24/7 to talk confidentially with anyone experiencing abuse.

If you or someone you know may be the victim or the abuser in a toxic relationship and you wish to seek help, resources & information we are here for you. If you're questioning the healthiness of your relationship and have some concerns. Please reach out to **mybeatenheart.org** for online help and assistance.

Made in the USA
Columbia, SC
12 October 2020